BLACK, WHITE & the BLUES

Jazz & Blues, Soul & Ska in Post-War Portsmouth

Dave Allen

Moyhill Publishing

First Published in 2021 by Moyhill Publishing.

ISBN 978-1-913529-85-7

A CIP catalogue record for this book
is available from the British Library.

Moyhill Publishing,
1965 Davenport House, 261 Bolton Rd, Bury, Gtr. Manchester BL8 2NZ. UK.

List of Contents

Introduction

This book takes as its principal focus the impact of black American and to a lesser extent Caribbean music and musicians on the people of Portsmouth in the quarter-of-a-century from the end of the Second World War to the start of the 1970s.

In one respect it documents those visiting acts in chapters, each of which focuses mainly on a specific genre or style, and presented chronologically starting a century ago with jazz in New Orleans. From there it moves through the big bands, early blues and gospel recordings, bebop, rhythm & blues and rock & roll, moving on to 'cool' jazz, Motown, soul, ska and the ground-breaking guitar of Jimi Hendrix.

That is a fairly familiar historical structure, used here to organise the arbitrary order in which many of these musicians appeared in the city – Louis Armstrong for example came in 1962, shortly after two other great trumpeters, Dizzy Gillespie (1959) and Miles Davis (1960) but he clearly precedes them in historical significance and that is how the book is organised, with a chronological diary of the Portsmouth appearances at the back of the book.

But this is not merely a listing of great music and great musicians since it also seeks to place their music in the broader post-war context of huge changes in tastes and preferences among British musicians and audiences, nationally and locally. That will examine in particular how their performances were received by the city's critics and audiences and how more broadly their music, ranging through a variety of styles and genres, influenced British musicians from the bigger national names to the many local acts playing in the clubs, pubs and ballrooms on Portsea Island.

There is a pattern of sorts in this latter focus revealing that for some time post-war, white audiences, critics and musicians often preferred to look back in search of a notional 'authenticity' to the pre-war sounds and styles of New Orleans jazz, the big bands, and acoustic 'rural' blues and gospel. By contrast, only a minority engaged with the challenges of post-war bebop and beyond. or the perceived 'wildness' of mid-1950s rock & roll. Gradually, a new generation engaged with the more popular contemporary developments of soul, ska, Motown and rock although the innovations of other forms, notably post-1960 'avant-garde' or 'free' American jazz, were rarely more than the preference of a minority of fans.

The varied views and responses are reflected in some of the contemporary reviews of the visiting performances so that for example, local critical praise for Ellington, Ella Fitzgerald or the Motown Review must be weighed against criticisms of Miles Davis, Muddy Waters or the Modern Jazz Quartet. To what extent do these critical reviews reveal the quality of the performance at the time and how much do they tell us something of the city's culture in a period when for example, there were moves on the council to ensure that there would be no jazz (let alone 'pop') at the beautiful new Guildhall?

In some respects the list of great names that did appear is a tribute to those who worked to make the events happen as well as those who supported them, although this was an inconsistent tale with modern jazz having to fight particularly hard for its audience in what was (and is?) in many respects a culturally conservative city. This is perhaps to be expected when the principal economic driver was Her Majesty's Royal Navy, a rather different organisation from the Merchant variety and the ports where cultural interaction was rather more a matter of course in daily life.

Portsmouth is Britain's only island city with a population of around 200,000 and in the census of 2011 it revealed that fewer than 2% of its inhabitants were classed as black with around 90% as (mostly) white British or white 'other; in the period covered here that black percentage was probably lower. In addition to the Royal Navy there is nowadays business for the cross-channel ferry port but it is situated on the north-west corner of the city, and can be accessed directly from the M27, so because Portsmouth is an island on the southern edge of the country, it is not normally a place that people pass through, unless the Isle of Wight is their destination. Otherwise you visit for a specific purpose or you do not come and like many islands its population can be somewhat insular.

We know something about how Portsmouth was seen in the 1960s because in November 1968 *The Times* published a lengthy article under the title "Why Pompey is under a cloud", which revealed that among the 20 biggest cities in the country, Portsmouth had

- The highest suicide rate,
- The third highest illegitimacy rate,
- The highest county borough rate of children in care,
- High incidences of drug addiction and venereal disease,
- 2.9% unemployment, against 1.7% in the region, and 2.4% nationally.

The 1960s were a period of high employment, but even then, Portsmouth lagged behind many other places, and the article reported that 40% of male employees in the city worked in HM Dockyard, where the "wages are low and there is little competition for labour". The newer industries, like IBM were generally locating to the north of (and just off) the island which encouraged employees to move out of the city centre to the private and council estates. What the article failed to note was the extent through the 1960s to which the growing popularity of cheap continental holidays impacted on the city's seaside holiday resort area of Southsea, which had previously brought visitors, thereby supporting and enhancing the entertainment and leisure industries in the city. The end of National Service in the early 1960s and a steady decline in the size of the Royal Navy had a similar effect on potential audiences.

Prior to that however, the story told here is one of cultural enrichment that we can see in retrospect as remarkable, unprecedented and unmatched since. It is in that sense a celebratory tale, told on behalf of all of us who were lucky enough to experience it, and shared with anyone and everyone who might wish they had been here too.

Dave Allen
Old Portsmouth
July 2021

A Note on Style

The topics and terms used in a book with this subject matter demand a degree of care and sensitivity although it is for others to judge whether this has been achieved. The most obvious requirement is to deal accurately and respectfully with the question of race and I have chosen throughout to employ 'black' as the principal adjective in describing the main subjects – for example, black music or musician. In this my main point of reference has been the current online 'Style Guide' of the *Guardian,* which previously suggested black (and white) should be employed lower case only, as an adjective, as above. The current version offers more leeway in the use of black or Black, suggesting

> There is ongoing debate about the capitalisation of black, with some using it as a physical descriptor, others to describe a specific cultural group, therefore while generally lower case, if a subject, writer or editor of a story prefers to use Black then that choice should be respected.

I have chosen to stay with the lower-case initialisation, noting that it is the approach used by David Olusoga in his fine book *Black and British: A Forgotten History.* I hope it will be satisfactory.

In the matter of sources and styles I have chosen to forsake the familiar conventions of academic referencing. Early drafts of this tale were weighed down by footnotes which I felt might discourage the general reader, or those new to the subject. Instead I have written with few quotations or references and where they do appear the source might be found through the single bibliography at the back, which is not comprehensive but I hope will be useful both for indicating some of the key sources over the decades in my understanding of these topics and also as suggested reading for those who wish to go further.

In many cases I have quoted directly from the archives of the *Evening News,* available on film in the city's Central Library. Since they mostly refer to specific events and the articles appeared within a few days before or after, these are not difficult to locate. In those days, there were two 'writers' on the newspaper who would comment or run columns on popular music, under the pen-names 'Perdido' and the more pop-oriented 'Spinner' – a name which remained through the years under the authorship of a number of different writers. In addition, jazz and folk became briefly the province of a weekly column under another pseudonym 'the 'Jazzmen', while some specific reviews were published under initials such as MRH, SR, JN and BAK. Whoever they were, I thank them for their endeavours; they are invaluable.

In addition to the matter of initialisation, I have followed the *Guardian Style Guide* in some simple matters, so always Britain (not UK), bebop rather than Be Bop (etc) and the Beatles (etc.) rather than The Beatles – differing only in respect of their suggested single word rock'n'roll, because I prefer it as rock & roll. Finally there is the matter of 'rhythm & blues' or 'R&B' where it advises the latter abbreviation can be used "whether you are listening to Bo Diddley or Beyoncé, although only the former style should be referred to as rhythm and blues". Beyoncé is of course too contemporary to appear here but while I use the full spelling in the 'Bo Diddley' sense of post-war black American music, R&B is employed in two ways; when referring to the specialist charts of record sales in the USA or Britain, or when referring specifically to the British version in the 1960s – for example the music of the Rolling Stones, Alexis Korner, Manfred Mann and others.

Acknowledgements

I would like to thank Frank Hurlock, Jerry Allen (no relation) and Ted Laker who were there in the early days, making things happen – and to Ted and Jerry for their memories, contained within, to which I'll add Ted's younger brother Graham who sent the diaries and kept me informed about the Jazz Train and the early R&B days.

As ever, my thanks to my good friend Mick Cooper, whose efforts over many years, documenting Pompey's past, have made an invaluable contribution to this publication.

Thanks too to Paul 'Smiler' Anderson whose publications and other endeavours around the Mod scene have helped to keep the Pompey sixties alive.

Finally my thanks as ever to David Cronin for all his work and expertise in getting this into print and out there, and to my wife Lou, always supportive when I disappear under a mound of books and albums. If I missed anyone, my apologies and belated thanks.

O N E

Back to New Orleans

Louis Armstrong, 'Kid' Ory, Fats Waller, The British Revival

On 3 May 1962 Portsmouth Guildhall hosted what is still one of its most historic events, a concert by the legendary jazz trumpeter and singer Louis Armstrong. Armstrong had performed in Britain 30 years earlier but this was his first visit to Portsmouth and he brought a band with its own heritage: trombonist 'Trummy' Young, was previously with Earl Hines, Jimmie Lunceford and Charlie Barnett; New Orleans clarinettist Joe Barensbourg had ten years with Kid Ory; trumpeter 'Billy' Cronk came from Tommy Dorsey's Band; pianist 'Billy' Kyle was from the bands of Lucky Millinder and Tiny Bradshaw, and with them were drummer Danny Barcelona, and 25-year-old vocalist Jewel Brown. In an earlier concert on the same tour, the *Melody Maker* described Armstrong as "an outstanding success, (who) twisted like a youngster, got a great reception … and used up 25 handkerchiefs". For most British jazz fans with a preference for the traditions of New Orleans around 40 years earlier, he was *the* great figure, the accomplished musician whose late 1920s recording ensembles, the 'Hot Fives' and 'Hot Sevens', brought a new emphasis on soloing within the traditional ensemble. He was also the singer whose timing influenced a generation, while scat-singing his way into the history of the vocal arts.

Of that particular concert, Portsmouth's *Evening News* reviewer 'MRH' praised each member of the group as "a superb instrumentalist" with timing that was "spot on" reporting also that Armstrong, having played for well-over an hour to both sold-out houses, was told by the Guildhall's manager (David Evans) as the evening reached its close to "play as long as he liked", after which his encores ran for nearly half-an-hour and the venue arranged the late-night buses to be available for the late finish. MRH described how Armstrong played many "favourites" including "The Saints", "Blueberry Hill", "Mack the Knife", "Now You Has Jazz", and "Georgia", one of three songs by Jewel Brown, although his vocal preference was for Armstrong's version of the spiritual "Nobody Knows the Trouble I've Seen".

In Britain Armstrong had been the key figure in the post-war years for most of the British jazz bands and their followers involved in the 1940s jazz revival; he enjoyed a couple of British top ten hit singles in the 1950s (and two more in the 1960s) while in the first two years of the new decade he released two British Top Twenty albums which drew on his roots 40-plus years earlier: *Satchmo plays King Oliver* (1960) and *Jazz Classics* (1961). Cornet player Joe 'King' Oliver (1885-1938) to whom Armstrong paid tribute on that album had been playing in New Orleans from the early years of the century and in the 1920s was Armstrong's rival, leading his famous Creole Jazz Band, although he and Armstrong also played together.

Oliver also played at one time in the band led by trombonist Edward 'Kid' Ory who had been one of the members of Louis Armstrong's legendary 'Hot Five', which along with the larger 'Hot Seven' was brought together in Chicago between 1925-1930, solely for the purposes of recording sides for the Okeh label. 'Kid' Ory was still performing during the 1950s and while he was not an international draw like Armstrong, in October

1959, a few months after Portsmouth Guildhall re-opened, his New Orleans Jazz Band appeared there in concert. Another man who contributed to those historic Chicago recordings, pianist Earl Hines also appeared at the Guildhall (March 1967) in the package tour 'Jazz from the Swinging Era' alongside trumpeter Buck Clayton – formerly of the Count Basie Band – and veteran saxophonist Bud Freeman (born 1906) previously a member of the bands led by Benny Goodman and Tommy Dorsey.

Another event reaching way back into jazz history came in June 1964 in the Guildhall's Small Concert Hall – now the studio – when an Oxfam Charity Event presented 'Kid' Thomas Valentine and Emmanuel Paul, veteran American jazzmen with a combined age of 128 years. They were backed by Kid Martyn's New Orleans Ragtime Band including local trumpeter Cuff Billett in what the 'Jazzmen' in their weekly column in Portsmouth's *Evening News*, described as "a joyous concert". Their correspondent Ted Laker also wrote to praise 'Kid' Thomas who "shook the audience … into a cheerful responsive mood with his brand of showmanship". Trumpeter Thomas from Louisiana, had grown up in New Orleans and from the mid-1920s played in a band popular with local dancers in the city's suburb of Algiers, Louisiana. Paul, slightly younger than Valentine, was one of the first tenor saxophonists to play regularly in New Orleans and like the other visiting American musicians offered a taste of jazz as it had been in and around New Orleans and Chicago 40 and more years earlier.

Drummer Kid Martyn's British band recorded at least one LP and in addition to Billett included Peter Dyer (trombone) Bill Greenow (clarinet), Graham Patterson (piano), John Coles (banjo), and Terry Knight (bass). Their name, 'Kid' Martyn's New Orleans Ragtime Band told you what you needed to know if you went to one of their gigs, and they played as the headline act pretty regularly around Portsmouth in the early 1960s, notably at the Rendezvous Club opened by Ernie Sears in an old church in Ashburton Road in 1960, when it was said to be the only Saturday night jazz club in the city. The locals were not too keen on young people having fun at the top end of the road leading from Kimbells Ballroom, Osborne Road and so over the five years of its life the Rendezvous Club moved around to various Southsea locations, including St Paul's Road, the Dockyard Club (Onslow Road), and South Parade Pier, before crossing Fratton Bridge to settle in Kingston Road's Oddfellows Hall in early 1964, where its traditional jazz policy shifted to the increasingly popular British R&B scene. That is a tale for later.

There had been an audience for New Orleans-style jazz in Britain at least back to 1919, when the (all white) Original Dixieland Jazz Band visited the country, as did Will Marion Cook's Southern Syncopators, including the soon to be renowned soprano saxophonist Sidney Bechet. The 1920s are often called 'The Jazz Age' although in terms of music that was a fairly loose description, especially in Britain, while for all its popularity among mostly younger people it was often viewed with hostility by those who feared the culture that surrounded it – and it was often subjected to racist comments even initially in the weekly *Melody Maker*, launched in 1926, which post-war would be a strong supporter of jazz,

Even where there was a preference for a certain kind of 'jazz' in Britain it might often be for the melodic but predictable dance bands, exemplified by the BBC Dance Orchestra led first by Jack Payne, and from 1932 by Henry Hall, although during the early 1930s other American jazz musicians came to Britain including Buddy Berigan, Muggsy Spanier, and in 1932 Louis Armstrong followed one year later by Duke Ellington. While neither Ellington nor Armstrong visited Portsmouth in those pre-war days, both would perform there in the 1960s.

Unfortunately Britain's Musicians' Union began to express concerns that visiting American bands were taking work from their British counterparts, so although jazz was growing in popularity the Union persuaded the Ministry of Labour to impose a ban on most visiting American bands for around twenty years, until eventually they came to a reciprocal arrangement, which in 1956 saw the popular British Ted Heath Band tour America in exchange for Stan Kenton's American Orchestra. Kenton's band opened to a blaze of publicity in London in March 1956, and shortly after appeared at Southsea seafront's Savoy Ballroom – unusually in a seated concert. It was normally *the* Portsmouth dance venue which Heath's band knew very well as regular visitors to Portsmouth through the 1950s.

Despite the ban, there were a few exceptions over the 20 years, mainly for solo artists who could appear as cabaret or variety acts, and one of them visited Portsmouth for the first week of May 1939, opening two days after Pompey's football-ers had won the FA Cup for the first time. He was Thomas 'Fats' Waller, appearing in a Variety Show at the Hippodrome just south of the Guildhall Square opposite the Theatre Royal. The show would seem rather odd today since along with the Hippodrome's resident Orchestra, came Tyrolean acrobats, Australian dancers, comedy cyclists, a juggler, "Tit-Bits of 1939", three comedians, Sylvestre "the Sunshade Maker" (?) and "the first visit to Portsmouth of the World's Greatest Rhythm Pianist, 'Fats' Waller, Master of Swing". There were two shows every night through the week, and for Fats Waller, a major black American performer, it was part of a tour of the country during which time he composed "The London Suite". During his short life he was a hugely popular and commercially successful performer and, while Paul Robeson performed on South Parade Pier in 1930, Waller was almost certainly the first major black jazz artist to visit Portsmouth.

Whether this anticipated a growing audience for jazz in the immediate aftermath we shall never know of course, for the world of light and live entertainment in Britain was to be somewhat curtailed over the next six years, not least in the Royal Naval and Dockyard city of Portsmouth. By the time the war had ended, the Hippodrome was no more, demolished in a bombing raid that also destroyed much of the Guildhall just a short distance away. It would be twenty years after Waller's visit before the Guildhall was rebuilt and reopened but the Hippodrome never was – that site now houses Sainsbury's. Light entertainment on Southsea's seafront was also curtailed, particularly in 1944 in the build-up to D-Day but after the war Billy Butlin took over the Savoy Buildings, including the Ballroom, opposite South Parade Pier and during the 1950s in particular it became the leading local venue in the growing popularity of jazz and other light entertainments.

Jazz in Britain over that post-war period split into two broad and sometimes competing groups, although there was further factionalism within them. In simple terms there were on the one hand the modernists and also those musicians – initially often amateurs – who looked back fondly to the New Orleans of King Oliver, Kid Ory, Louis Armstrong and others, and set about 'reviving' that music. That camp also spilt between those who wished to draw particularly on Armstrong's legendary commercial recordings of the late 1920s and those, following Ken Colyer, who looked back even further, seeking a kind of 'authenticity' in the traditions of New Orleans during the First World War.

Unlike Armstrong's Hot Fives and Hot Sevens, there were few recordings of the earlier New Orleans jazz, which presented a particular challenge for those who wished to play it, although they knew that the frontline instruments that sat on a rhythm section of drums, banjo, and maybe piano were mostly trumpet, trombone and clarinet. Saxophones were rare, sometimes the bass would be provided by a tuba and the sound was built on ensemble playing rather than solos. Armstrong's recordings by contrast included solos by most of the ensemble and with around 80 recorded tracks, source material was plentiful for young British musicians – even in the days of 78rpm records with just two tracks on each. Among the recordings that were performed regularly by British post-war musicians were "Willie the Weeper"; "Hear Me Talkin' to Ya"; "St James Infirmary"; "Twelfth Street Rag"; "Muskrat Ramble" and "After You've Gone". The recording of "Heebie Jeebies" includes Armstrong's famous scatting section, reputedly because the words fell from the music stand during the session which in those days could not be stopped and redone – the disc was already cutting. Was his improvised scatting the first example of this wordless singing? Possibly not, but the legend became fact, and scat singing became part of the repertoire of many fine vocalists, not least twenty years later during the heyday of bebop. "Mahogany Hall Stomp" meanwhile was one of those tracks that gave its name to the particular dance favoured by the followers of the British revivalist bands, the stomp – a two-person dance not unlike jiving but with a heavier emphasis on the heavy rhythmic foot movements.

A number of Armstrong's Chicago recordings were blues, such as "Wild Man Blues", "Potato Head Blues", "Weary Blues", "Basin Street Blues" and the most famous composition by WC Handy, an up-tempo, 'Latin' rendering of "St Louis Blues" with Armstrong on vocals. This link between jazz and blues was emphasised by Armstrong's presence on 1925 New York recordings by the 'Empress of the Blues' Bessie Smith, including her version of "St Louis Blues", "Reckless Blues", "Sobbin' Hearted Blues", "Cold in Hand Blues", "You've Been a Good Old Wagon", Nashville Women's Blues" and a staple of many post-war British jazz and folk-blues musicians, "Careless Love". Armstrong was not the only major jazz musician to accompany Bessie Smith – others included Sidney Bechet, Coleman Hawkins (who came to Portsmouth), James P Johnson, Benny Goodman and Fletcher Henderson. Bessie Smith's recordings were also an important source for George Melly, one of the first post-war British blues singers who sang with Mick Mulligan's Magnolia Jazz Band; they appeared regularly in Portsmouth through the 1950s and Melly later wrote a highly amusing memoir of those days, *Owning Up*.

Britain's New Orleans 'revival' bands initially performed in clubs and pubs, mostly playing for dancers as we can see in the British documentary film *Momma Don't Allow* by Karel Reisz and Tony Richardson filmed in Wood Green Jazz Club, London in 1954. The evening's entertainment is provided by Chris Barber's leading British band, but focuses more on the dancing audience, including an amusing sequence when an upper-class group arrive and dance ineptly. The 'regulars', shown as 'ordinary' young working people, have rather more impressive moves.

Dancing to live bands was often an important aspect of pre and post-war live entertainment in the mid-twentieth century but another important element in the growth of an audience for jazz and eventually other black music in Britain came through the collecting and careful study of records and discographies despite their limited availability in those years. The majority of live jazz acts playing in Portsmouth in the 1950s were white,

British, but hearing and recreating or interpreting recordings by the original performers became increasingly possible from the 1930s onwards, as in Portsmouth and elsewhere clubs were set up and offered lectures and record recitals presented by and shared between the 'serious' fans.

So it was, for example, that in January 1951 Frank Hurlock, an influential local figure in jazz, blues and folk music, gave a talk to Portsmouth Jazz Club, entitled "Hurlock's Dixieland Jazz Band"; a fictitious story about the progress of a jazz group, illustrated with recordings by popular New Orleans and Chicago jazzmen. One month later, members at the local 'Club Dixie' meeting, elected one of the new stars of British jazz, trumpeter Humphrey Lyttleton, as their President, while the Portsmouth Rhythm Club met at the Sir Robert Peel 'pub' in the city centre. During those same early months of 1951, live performers included a week on South Parade Pier with the band of trumpeter Kenny Baker; traditional jazz pioneers the Crane River Band at the Savoy Ballroom, and at the same venue something more 'modern' with the Johnny Dankworth Seven. Whether Cleo Laine was present we cannot be sure but she was advertised twelve months later during a period when Chris Barber's New Orleans Jazz Band and the Humphrey Lyttleton Band both visited the Savoy. Lyttleton tended to be more inventive and less constrained by the British jazz 'camps' of the period although he would dismay New Orleans 'die-hards' by featuring a saxophonist (Bruce Turner) and embracing some more modern sounds and styles, although they were never a bebop band. That style was the preference of many professional British musicians who often earned a living in the dance bands, but as we shall see, played contemporary 'modern' jazz after-hours.

One of the first black acts to visit the city, Ray Ellington & his Quartet, came to the Savoy Ballroom in January 1950 and the South Parade Pier in April 1951. Ellington's father was American, but Ray was born in London and his quartet drew on sometimes comedic pre-rock & roll 'jump' blues and unusually featured an electric guitar. They would later gain national attention as the house band for the Goons' popular BBC radio show. In July 1952, the black American singer Adelaide Hall (1901-1993), who had moved to Paris in 1935 and then Britain in 1938, appeared at the Theatre Royal; in her days in the USA she had recorded with Fats Waller and most famously with Duke Ellington on "Creole Love Call" and other sides. A few months after her visit, again at the Theatre Royal, the Deep River Boys, an American gospel and rhythm & blues act, gave Portsmouth an early taste of doo-wop, while visiting there in 1954 was the black cabaret star Leslie 'Hutch' Hutchinson. He was born in Grenada and settled in England after a period in New York.

There was a fascinating week-long show at the King's Theatre in April 1955, a production of the Mervyn Nelson musical *Jazz Train* from the United States on the opening week of a nationwide tour. In a preview *the Evening News* described "a swift-moving cavalcade of jazz in the Negro style" with a mainly American cast plus other recruits "from many parts of the world". Nelson took the idea from the "jazz-type of music that was popular in the twenties", while working on a production of *The Boyfriend* and set his production as an "old-style railroad train with coaches representing the various stages in the evolution of jazz". Among the cast members, American-born, British-based actress Bertice Reading played Bessie Smith singing "Frankie & Johnny" and when Nelson was told "Southsea has the most critical audiences outside London" he replied "That's fine – let's go there". Sadly there was no review, although Graham Laker was taken and decades later it had stayed with him:

I was only six years old when I saw it but can still remember parts of it very clearly – the colourful men's shirts in pink, yellow and bright green, the rendition of "Frankie and Johnny", using a ladder so that when Frankie was shot she slid down it – it all made quite an impression on me. It was very colourful and energetic and must have been way ahead of its time. (It's) surprising that it's not better remembered or appreciated".

Through the 1950s most of the main British jazz acts played in the city. In addition to those mentioned already came Freddie Randall's Band, Nat Gonella & his Georgians, the Cy Laurie Band, the High Curley Stompers (including future skiffle star Chas McDevitt), the Mick Mulligan Band with George Melly, Ken Colyer's Jazzmen and Kenny Ball's Jazzmen – plus 'modern' acts including the Orchestras of Ronnie Scott, Tubby Hayes and Johnny Dankworth and British-based Jamaican saxophonist Joe Harriott. Alan Zeffert's amusing memoir of those days in Portsmouth (1988) revealed that he had become a teenage 'bop' fan as the 1940s drew to a close and went frequently to the Savoy on Friday nights. In the modern field he added to the above named his admiration for the Tito Burns Sextet and the Vic Lewis Band ("Britain's own Kenton") including saxophonist Kathy Stobart, but he recalled less fondly one night when the Ronnie Scott Orchestra seemed intent on playing standard 'pop' tunes of the time. Zeffert, in his favourite spot by the stage called out "How about some jazz then?", to which Ronnie Scott's response was to collect a few shillings from his future club partner Pete King, hand Zeffert his 4/- (20p) entrance money and tell him to "piss off"!

Alan Zeffert had other revealing tales from those days. He had for example attended the first meetings of the Portsmouth Jazz Club in 1947, organised by Frank Hurlock, which attracted a small audience and was soon disbanded – but not before Zeffert realised it was going to cater principally for the "mouldy fygges", the traditional jazz fans whose preferences went back to New Orleans. Instead, he decided to organise a Jazz Records Club while in the sixth form at Portsmouth Grammar School – in those days a Direct Grant not Independent Grammar School. He provided the record player and records, but the Headmaster fearful of the response from his largely middle-class parents banned it. Zeffert had departed when a decade later a similar effort at the school by a new cohort elicited the same response although the boys' response then was to refuse to sing in assembly. Zeffert also recounted that when preparing for his Higher School Certificate examination in English he had responded to a requirement to write a critique of a musical work of art and chose Duke Ellington's extended historical concert piece "Black, Brown and Beige". His teacher praised the working calling it a "splendid effort" before adding that it would not pass "because of the subject matter". In Britain's 1940s & 1950s, jazz encouraged strong feelings and opinions, whether from those opposed to it, or from within the sectarian boundaries of the aficionados.

Most evenings with a 'star' national act included local support, from one of the dance bands and there were some special events such as the Jazz Band Ball at the Savoy Ballroom in August 1950 with music from the assorted bands of Humphrey Lyttleton, Mike Daniels, Chris Barber, Mick Mulligan and Portsmouth's Benny Freedman. Two years later the three jazz bands at the South Parade Pier were Mick Mulligan and his New Magnolia Band, Chris Barber and his New Orleans Jazzmen and the Crane River Jazz Band.

On Monday 8 June 1959, almost exactly 15 years after troops left Portsmouth for the D-Day invasion of France, HM Queen

Elizabeth II came to the rebuilt Guildhall to declare it open. The celebrations on the first evening comprised a classical concert in the new 2,000-seater hall, led by the Master of the Queen's Music Sir Arthur Bliss, then on the next night there was a sell-out concert by the Chris Barber Jazz Band with their Irish blues singer Ottilie Patterson. This was not uncontroversial however – in the previous year, *the Evening News* quoted Councillor Mrs R Mack:

Jazz at the Guildhall? Oh no … I should definitely be opposed … I think Portsmouth should aspire to something greater. As a holiday resort Southsea has already been dragged down enough. I think it is time Portsmouth had some culture – whether the public likes it or not. The Guildhall should present first-class classical music.

Despite that view, in the early years, jazz was a frequent visitor to the rebuilt Guildhall. *The Evening News* reviewed the opening jazz concert with the headline "4,000 Feet Tap to Barber's Jazz" and opening with "Jazz, the music of New Orleans gaming houses and Chicago speakeasies gained civic reception in Portsmouth last night". There was a reference to the "controversy" of the previous year but the report suggested that with this concert "the dream of local jazz enthusiasts came true". Of the Barber Band there was a not untypical critical response of that time in the suggestion "there is nothing clever or subtle about (their) brand of jazz" but the event was nonetheless "a complete and exciting success". The concert programme indicated a big selection of possible tunes from which they played among others, "Bourbon Street Parade", "Panama Rag", "Blue Turning Grey Over You" and "Million Dollar Secret" featuring Ottilie Patterson, although they ignored their recent hit record, a version of Sidney Bechet's "Petite Fleur".

The following day's *Evening News* ran an editorial which considered the various opening events at the Guildhall, and asked, "Is Portsmouth Musical?" It suggested every night so far had been an "outstanding success" thanks to the "hard work of a few" and added hopes that the city would now become a major musical venue which it had "ceased to be" during the 1930s. Post-war it had become rather more a centre for light entertainment and variety shows, not least in response to the summer holidaymakers who came to Southsea. For them the major events were probably dancing at the Savoy or the summer seasons across the road on South Parade Pier, which lasted a week or sometime longer. During that heatwave summer of 1959 the pier opened with the Beverly Sisters and comedian Arthur Haynes, followed by Billy Cotton & his Band; Arthur Askey; Ted Ray; Bob Monkhouse and Yana for six weeks; Top Ten vocalist Dickie Valentine, and finally 'crooner' Jimmy Young.

As the 1960s loomed, the Guildhall played host to concerts by another popular British jazz band led by Humphrey Lyttleton, and from America, the Dave Brubeck Quartet and a number of black American acts including the Dizzy Gillespie Quintet, Kid Ory's New Orleans Band, Buck Clayton's All Stars and the Modern Jazz Quartet. *The Evening* News reported that the Kid Ory Band gave "an energetic and spirited programme of traditional favourites" with trumpeter Henry 'Red' Allen taking lead on most numbers, while they featured two singers Ory's "pleasant guttural singing" ("Bill Bailey" and others) and drummer Alton Redd on "Careless Love" and "Basin Street Blues".

The MJQ concert in December 1959 was promoted by the National Jazz Federation and while they appeared without any support act *the Melody Maker* reported (October 1959) that at the "special request" of their pianist John Lewis,

British saxophonists Ronnie Ross and Joe Harriott "will be featured as solo guest stars" with the quartet. These dates as the 1950s drew to a close heralded the start of a wonderful decade of visits to Portsmouth by black American, British and Caribbean musicians.

In Portsmouth, there was clearly an appetite for the historic jazz styles, although contemporary critics were not always convinced by the home-grown acts – even the best-known of them. Bob Dawbarn in the *Melody Maker* in 1962 for example suggested grudgingly "even Chris Barber's severest critics must surely be grateful to him for giving us the opportunity to hear so many fine American guest artists on his shows", adding, Barber "tends to get the blame for the sins of the entire revival movement and most of the band's faults apply to just about every other local New Orleans group". He preferred the band ("at its best") on their "highly-arranged passages", with the exception of their one attempt at ragtime, "The Entertainer".

There were nonetheless plenty of fans 'out there' and the fondness for the New Orleans style was reflected in Portsmouth's clubs and pubs where in the late-1950s and early-1960s a range of jazz might be found. The venues included the peripatetic Rendezvous Club (1960-65), and Ricky's in Goldsmith Avenue which like the Railway Hotel behind Fratton Station mixed old and 'new' jazz with rock & roll nights. Pubs included the Cobden Arms in Arundel Street, the Star, Lake Road, the Air Balloon in Buckland, the Pure Drop in Middle Street and the Cellar Club in Hampshire Terrace (later the Indigo Vat, more recently Scandals) – in the latter many recordings of New Orleans-style local jazz bands were made during the mid-1960s. Jazz was also still being featured at the Savoy and on South Parade Pier, with the top British names visiting those venues and the Guildhall.

For the most part the pub and club events featured local or national, usually London-based, bands although local musician and jazz lover Edward 'Ted' Laker recalled an evening when New Orleans trombonist Louis Nelson guested at the Portland Hotel, Kent Road with Barry Martyn's Band, and on another occasion New Orleans trumpeter Kid Sheik (George Colar) of the Preservation Hall Jazz Band played to an enthusiastic crowd at Fratton's Railway Hotel. 'Ted' Laker, recorded his involvement in a series of diaries and later reminiscences of those days, including how, in the early 1960s he joined the Commodore New Orleans Jazz Band playing around the many local jazz venues of the time such as the Winchester Arms, Railway Hotel, Fishers Club etc.

In the mid-1950s Ted bought a second-hand trumpet in Foreman's, Lake Road, and took lessons with Stan Emptage the lead trumpet in local band and Savoy regulars the Benny Freedman Orchestra. Ted upgraded his instrument at Courtney & Walker's, at the time in Arundel Street, and answered an advertisement in the local paper seeking members to form a 'New Orleans' jazz band. They rehearsed regularly in the Winchester Arms off New Road, another live music venue to this day, and made their debut after six months, following that gig with others at local church halls and social clubs. They also ventured out to Leigh Park and Portchester and then to two important local venues, the Railway Hotel in Fratton and Hampshire Terrace.

After personnel changes they moved rehearsals to the Old House at Home in Locksway Road and members of the band also 'sat in' on pub sessions at the Star in Lake Road, the Auckland Arms off Osborne Road, the Pure Drop in Sackville Street and the Cobden in Arundel Street, which is where they enjoyed weekly sessions by one of the leading local groups, Cuff

Billet's Vieux Carre Jazz Band – named after a famous square in New Orleans. According to his diary Ted welcomed in the 1960s watching the band there at his "first jazz session" of the sixties on Wednesday 6 January, and from those days, Ted remembered fondly "so many pubs held jazz sessions, you could just amble from one to another". From 1960-1963 Ted Laker kept diaries, notes and advertisements from the local paper for many live events, too many to list them all here but notable occasions included regular local gigs by bassist/drummer Derek Adye's New Orleans Jazz Band', the "lovely" Josephine Collinson singing with the Bourbon Street Six, Pedro Harris's Pine City Stompers and a newly formed 'Folk Blues Association' at the Railway Hotel in the spring of 1963.

Despite this positive picture, in early 1960 George Turner, manager of the Savoy for some years told *the Evening News* that styles were "changing" with "jazz clubs closing down" and his ballroom going back to bands playing strict tempo (waltz, foxtrot etc.) for the dancers – he did however add that when it came to jazz, 'Trad' was OK "because you can dance to it" and to bear this out in April he presented Mick Mulligan's band with blues singer George Melly and in June Al Fairweather & Sandy Brown. In 1962, just ahead of the beat group explosion, the Savoy continued to present various traditional jazz acts including the Temperance Seven, and bands led by Terry Lightfoot and Acker Bilk.

It's possible that George Turner's comments were wishful thinking. By the spring, Portsmouth's own Le Vieux Carre Jazz Band described in the 'paper as playing "the finest 'Trad' in the area" were touring Holland while a group of art students in the Crescent City Jazz Band had outgrown the Conservative Hall and were moving on to a new venue. There were advertisements for Saturday nights of "Blues & Boogie" with the John White

Trio, Derek Adye's Jazz Band were playing the Railway Hotel on Fridays, and in mid-summer the pre-war British celebrity trumpeter Nat Gonella, now living in Gosport, appeared at Milton's Oyster House. Elsewhere, 'Old Time' dancing was encouraged at the Guildhall (March 1960) with Ivy Benson's all-woman Orchestra – "Evening Dress invited".

Less positively, in the summer the Summa Cum Laude Club closed through "lack of support" although the Rendezvous was now well established. As 1960 drew to a close *The Evening News* surveyed the world of popular music, with no inkling of what was just around the corner, and concluded jazz – traditional and modern – "has never had it so good" with well-run clubs locally, and good publicity. Not for the last time, there were reservations about the Guildhall as a venue, suggesting it was "not in fashion", although the recent 'Jazz at the Philharmonic' show – despite the final 'jam' session being a "complete waste of time and talent" – had perhaps "provided the cure". Elsewhere in 1961 *the Evening News* reported that while a year previously there had been six jazz clubs in the area now, "in keeping with the ever increasing popularity of jazz, there are twelve". In addition to the smaller pubs and clubs, Ted Laker and his pals also went to the big-name jazz events on South Parade Pier, especially on Sunday evenings, with Friday nights often spent at the Savoy. Ted was a particular fan of Ken Colyer whose band "played as many dates as possible in-and-around the area".

Ted also recalled Saturday mornings in the House of Wax record shop in Lake Road discussing second-hand "finds", as Frank Hurlock would check orders – decades later he ran a collectors' room upstairs in Orpheus Records, Marmion Road, a shop selling only classical, jazz and blues albums – no 'pop'. Ted enjoyed fruitful searches too, in Gosport, in the Petersfield Book Shop attic, in a junk shop in Lake Road overseen by an "eccentric Australian", and for new records there were among others, Ernest Wyatt's, who was a pioneer for the new LPs, Titmus's, in Arundel Street and Charles Hill in Marmion Road.

Kimbells did its best to warm up the bitter winter in January 1963, opening a new jazz club on Sunday nights with the Downtown Syncopators and Crescent City Jazz band – entry was 3/6d (18p) with membership 1/- (5p), while the Rendezvous re-located (again) to South Parade Pier, starting with the Rodney Foster Jazzmen from Ireland. But while the fans were busy going to gigs, in their *Evening News* weekly 'Offbeat' column, the 'Jazzmen' accused British 'Trad' of "trying to murder itself" by selling out to 'Tin Pan Alley'. The abbreviation 'Trad' as opposed to 'traditional' or 'revivalist' jazz had become a term of abuse among most jazz fans of the old New Orleans style and as examples of the 'sell-out', the 'Jazzmen' cited Acker Bilk's "Stranger on the Shore" and Kenny Ball's "Midnight in Moscow" which were repetitious but commercially successful because if "you take the jazz out of 'Trad', you have a selling sound", despite it being "heart-breaking" for the "purists". They did however also seek an alternative to the currently popular "stodgy New Orleans line-up".

One interesting alternative which anticipated changes hardly guessed at in January 1963 came at the Rendezvous where the familiar Bourbon Street Six with singer Jo Collinson shared the bill not with another traditional jazz band but with what was billed as "Britain's top ballad and blues duo", with an emphasis on blues, guitarist and singer Gerry Lockran and Royd Rivers on harmonica; a kind of British version of Sonny Terry & Brownie McGhee. The pair would return within a month and would appear subsequently on Railway Hotel folk nights. But as the ice melted and spring 1963 approached, the Beatles' "Please Please Me" made its way up the charts, 'Trad' slipped out of the top ten, and the Jazzmen breathed a sigh of relief as "the 'Trad' boom quietly died", after which they believed standards rose for jazz which was "escaping the net of commercialism". One consequence, however, reported in the *Evening News,* was that local music shops like Courtney & Walkers or Bennett's noted a decline in the sales of traditional jazz instruments – and of course an increase in the demand for electric guitars.

Loyal fans of traditional jazz remained nonetheless, while the major acts continued to appear from time-to-time in concert, ballrooms and festivals, on radio and television, records were released, or discovered and re-released, and the smaller clubs continued to provide opportunities for local musicians and their followers. By 1963 Portsmouth's 'traditional jazz' Rendezvous Club had only a few months to go before it was reinvented to cater for the new rhythm & blues sounds but the Cellar Club in Hampshire Terrace, was often busy with some of the best local jazz musicians. One of those, trumpeter Cuff Billett travelled in Ken Colyer's footsteps to New Orleans in 1963 where he sat in with some of the city's jazz musicians, reporting they "played as they have always played"; he found the experience "extraordinary" and "exhilarating". Giving his kind of jazz a boost were the students at the recently opened Highbury Technical College who opened a new jazz club where they presented the Solent City Jazz Band, Gerry Brown's Jazzmen, the Back O'Town Syncopators and the Bourbon Street Six.

In August 1964 the 'Jazzmen' took to the case again. With guitar groups now ruling roost in British popular music they praised the Alex Welsh Band for playing "great roaring Chicago jazz" and more generally noted that the recent British bands that survived the demise of the 'Trad' boom "play now with splendid defiance, greater vitality and far more skill". Sadly, few of the younger generation of music fans noticed the latest manifestation of the Dunkirk spirit; instead they went dancing to the latest pop records at the newly opened Locarno Ballroom which cost £250,000 and even offered lunchtime sessions 'Off the Record'.

T W O

It Don't Mean a Thing

Duke Ellington, Ella Fitzgerald, Count Basie, Dorsey & Herman

From the earliest days of jazz in New Orleans and the first recordings of jazz and blues acts, white bands seized opportunities to draw upon black American musical styles in building their careers. Two of the earliest and best known in the USA, the Original Dixieland Jazz Band (ODJB) and the Paul Whiteman Orchestra exemplified two approaches which jazz musicians would pursue through the following decades. The first was a small-group ensemble, with a front line and improvising soloists, while the other was a large Orchestra offering original arrangements of popular and sometimes newly creative music – and in Whiteman's case his Orchestra at times included fine instrumentalists such as Bix Beiderbecke (cornet) and guitarist Eddie Lang.

The white acts enjoyed considerable popularity and avoided many of the obvious difficulties of black artists, particularly but by no means exclusively in the southern states of the USA, but the small group approach would soon reach a higher level with the late 1920s Chicago recordings by Louis Armstrong, while the bigger orchestral sound would be taken on by two other important black American pianists and band leaders, Fletcher Henderson and Duke Ellington (1899-1974). As pianists, both men were influenced by the popular stride styles of James P Johnson, and Willie 'the Lion' Smith and as a band leader, Henderson entertained white patrons in New York's Roseland Ballroom for a decade. Ellington, frequently considered the finest of all the black American jazz composers and arrangers began leading his first small band in New York in the early 1920s and began recording in 1924, but the key moment came three years later when King Oliver declined a booking at Harlem's Cotton Club and Ellington, meeting the contractual requirements, expanded his band from six to 11-piece and like Henderson began entertaining the white audience, with the additional bonus of a weekly radio broadcast.

Ellington toured Britain in 1933 but was then subject to the same union restrictions as other American acts although he continued to write, perform and record in America. The early sound of Ellington's band was dominated by brass and included titles like "Creole Love Call", "Jubilee Stomp", "Black & Tan Fantasy", and "Hot & Bothered", while the sound became more sophisticated with the arrival of saxophonist Johnny Hodges in 1928 and in 1940 another major saxophonist Ben Webster. In 1956 an appearance at the Newport Jazz Festival boosted his popularity and as the ban was lifted, he began to tour Europe again – in 1958 his composition "The Queen's Suite" was a tribute to our recently crowned Queen Elizabeth II. Working with fellow composer Billy Strayhorn, Ellington composed the score for Otto Preminger's 1959 film *Anatomy of a Murder*, starring James Stewart, and two years later, *Paris Blues* with Steve McQueen and Sidney Poitier. While many of Ellington's hundreds of compositions were secular, with their roots in early jazz, blues and dance music in 1965 he presented what would be the first of his 'Sacred Concerts' and eighteen months later, in February 1967, the Duke Ellington Orchestra performed at Portsmouth Guildhall, his first and only visit to the city. It came exactly one year after

Ellington's performance in Coventry of a European Premiere concert of sacred music in the city's Cathedral, which had been destroyed by a firestorm in the Blitz. Whether Ellington knew that his venue and the surrounding area in Portsmouth had been similarly damaged we cannot know now – but it seems somewhat appropriate.

Ben Webster had departed when Ellington arrived in Portsmouth to open his latest British tour with two houses, but Hodges was still there during his second spell with the Orchestra as one of five saxophonists plus three trombones, four trumpets, string bass, drums and the leader on piano. Other names that night included Harry Carney (saxophone & clarinet), Cat Anderson (trumpet) and Duke's son Mercer Ellington, although his long-time collaborator Billy Strayhorn was absent, seriously ill; he died the following month in the USA. The report by BAK in the *Evening News* had the headline "Dazzling Duke Rides Hight at the Guildhall", suggested that the Orchestra "does not just glitter, it dazzles", and added "this is the finest band that jazz has seen", with "not a weak link". There was little mention of the repertoire except that on piano he offered "a light-hearted impersonation of Willie 'the Lion' Smith". Local musician Brian Cruickshank recalls the concert clearly: "the band opened the show from behind the closed curtains with "Take the 'A' Train", Ellington's theme tune. As the curtains opened the band turned on the volume – sensational. I can still remember the hairs on the back of my neck standing up. Brass seems to have that special resonance. I remember much of the concert. Fabulous".

During the tour, exactly two weeks after Portsmouth, Ellington played London's Royal Albert Hall with the London Philharmonic Orchestra and the following evening concluded the tour at Great St Mary's Church in Cambridge, with another

"Concert of Sacred Music." In a review of those two concluding concerts, Ronald Atkins (February 1967) wrote in the Guardian in general praise of Ellington's style as

> A concatenation of sounds, launched by the end of the 1920s and refined throughout the following decade to reach a sudden plateau of magnificence in the early forties. Throughout this period he produced works comparable to, but quite separate from, the achievements of contemporary straight music.

During the tour he also recorded a television broadcast in which the Orchestra played a set including: "Harlem", "Take the 'A' Train", "I got it bad and that ain't good", "Things ain't what they used to be", "Do nothin' till you hear from me", "Don't get around much anymore", "In a sentimental mood", "Mood Indigo", "I'm beginning to see the light", "Sophisticated Lady", "Caravan", "Solitude" and "I let a song go out of my heart".

Ellington led one of the great bands of the 1930s, the era of big bands and swing, but their degree of invention meant the band was by no means 'typical'. There were other bands from that era that also appeared at the Guildhall during the 1960s, most notably Count Basie's. His first scheduled visit in 1960 was cancelled due to a family bereavement but he came in April 1962 with the singers Lambert, Hendricks & Ross. By then Basie, another pianist influenced by the stride men, had led his band, originating in Kansas City, for more than a quarter-of-a-century and while they had gradually come to rely increasingly on careful arrangements, it was felt they still swung as much as any of the famous big bands. There was often a fine blues singer with the band, notably Jimmy Rushing or Joe Williams who both came to the Guildhall, and they also worked at times with Frank Sinatra and Ella Fitzgerald.

Other notable names from the world of the bigger bands who visited Portsmouth, included those led by Tommy Dorsey (February 1964 with Frank Sinatra jnr.), Woody Herman (July 1964) who on most of his tour attracted disappointing audiences but "swung like a dream", Maynard Ferguson (February 1969 with singers Jon Hendricks & Annie Ross), and Buddy Rich (April 1967) – plus The Dutch Swing College Band in June 1966, and "Jazz from the Swinging Era" with Bud Freeman, Earl Hines, Buck Clayton in March, 1967. When the Tommy Dorsey Orchestra came to Portsmouth, their Musical Director Sam Donahue told the *Evening News* "the kids are lost to us for ever … folk music … that's all they want". By the time they returned to the USA the Beatles and the following 'British Invasion' had arrived perhaps relegating 'folk' music to second place?

Five days after Ellington played Portsmouth Guildhall, Ella Fitzgerald joined the tour for some dates. Ella Fitzgerald worked with many leading jazz musicians through her long career; in August 1956 with Louis Armstrong she recorded one of the fairly new format vinyl long-playing albums *Ella and Louis* on the new Verve label, while in the autumn of 1957 she recorded a more ambitious four-LP 'box set' *Ella Fitzgerald Sings the Duke Ellington Song Book* partly with the Duke Ellington Orchestra, otherwise a small group featuring Ben Webster, Oscar Peterson, violinist Stuff Smith, guitarist Barney Kessell and others. She did not appear with Ellington in Portsmouth in 1967 but she had previously performed at the Guildhall in March 1960 when on a bill with the Jimmy Guiffre Trio and Shelley Manne and under the headline "Portsmouth Hails Top Jazz Singer", *the Evening News* reported "two terrific ovations from packed houses", adding, she "stunned" them. Ella Fitzgerald returned on three more occasions with the Oscar Peterson Trio in 1961, 1963 and April 1964, but on the last of those there was concern because while the second house sold out, the first house was cancelled with only 200 tickets sold. It was her last visit to the city, as pop gradually began to edge out jazz concerts at the venue.

In April 1960, there was also a rather special concert featuring Paul Robeson, a leading figure in black American 20th century culture, not just as a singer and actor but as a Civil Rights activist. His repertoire covered a variety of styles, including Americana, popular standards, classical music, European folk songs, political songs, poetry and spoken excerpts from plays. It was not Robeson's first visit to the city – in 1922 he travelled to Britain, arriving in Southampton before taking up a part in a play called *Voodoo,* starring Mrs Patrick Campbell. The rehearsals were at Southsea's King's Theatre and he stayed in lodgings around the corner for a while – and he returned to the city in 1930 for a concert on South Parade Pier. In an article in the *Evening News* in 1960, headlined "Robeson a Man of Sincerity" he was described being "proud of what as an Afro American and son of an ex-slave, he has been able to achieve".

Britain's Shirley Bassey visited the Guildhall on a number of occasions, first in February 1961, again in November with the Ken McIntosh Orchestra, in 1963 and 1964 with Matt Monro – the latter plus the John Barry Orchestra – in 1965 with Cyril Stapleton's Orchestra but sadly she missed 1963 when she toured the country with the American Orchestra of Nelson Riddle, who had arranged a number of successful albums in the 1950s for Capitol Records with Nat King Cole, Frank Sinatra, Dean Martin and others. While some of the leading American women vocalists of that crooning and swinging era appeared in Portsmouth, the leading men were mostly conspicuous by their absence.

There are various other tales to be told of big bands and jazz orchestras in Portsmouth. One is that during wartime the Glenn

Miller Orchestra is believed to have performed to servicemen in the city – possibly in a Hilsea barracks – another certainty that in 1956 the Stan Kenton Orchestra were the first American big band to play the city. They appeared at the Savoy as did most of the leading British dance bands of the period including those under the leadership of Ted Heath, Vic Lewis, Joe Loss, Tito Burns, Ray Ellington, Eric Delaney and Humphrey Lyttleton, plus the Squadronaires Dance Orchestra, and we have noted appearances by leading British modern jazz saxophonists Ronnie Scott, Johnny Dankworth (with Cleo Laine) and Tubby Hayes who brought their Orchestras to the seafront ballroom – on occasions some of these bands would also play South Parade Pier or less frequently the Theatre Royal. Early in 1960, Portsmouth band leader Benny Freedman celebrated his 10 years residency at the Savoy, headlining frequently and usually playing support on Friday nights which were known as "Radio Band Night".

Apart from Freedman, other local bands were led by Johnny Lyne, Wally Fry, Reg Bannistra and others. Their music was generally more dance-oriented than jazz *per se,* but there was at least a hint here-or-there – a tangential relationship to jazz and swing. Locally, a very good example of the formal expectations of the dance bands came with the achievement of Portsmouth's Johnny Lyne (Dance) Band who travelled to Manchester's Belle Vue Hall in October 1953 to compete in front of 7,000 fans in the *Melody Maker's* All-British championships. The subsequent newspaper report describes how the 15 competing bands from across Britain were required to play "one foxtrot, one waltz, one quickstep", and Tony Brown suggested that Lyne's band, runners-up in 1952, were "probably favourites". He heard in them, he suggested a "Sauter-Finegan influence" and felt that if they had a fault it was perhaps in the complexities of their arrangements. Lyne himself "quite some leader", switched from trumpet to clarinet, to alto saxophone, apparently playing the latter "very well in the fashionable cool manner" – despite the fixed programme, a reference to the modern jazz emerging from America's West Coast or recent recordings by Miles Davis. Johnny Lyne, whose address was given as 273 Arundel Street, where he had a music shop, was chosen as the competition's "outstanding musician" and his band were the overall Champions, enjoying the front-page headlines: "7,000 See Portsmouth Band win All-Britain".

There are existing recordings of the band which demonstrate careful arrangements befitting a band with three tenor saxophones, baritone, trumpet, trombone, piano, bass and drums – plus the leader. The Johnny Lyne Band was one of the accomplished local acts who played regularly around Portsmouth in the early 1950s but while band members like drummer Arthur Ward and pianist Bill Cole went on to lead their own bands for many years, Lyne seemed to disappear from Portsmouth after just a few more years leading his band. The recordings offer sufficient in the way of a syncopated feel and various solos to hear this as an example of Portsmouth dance band jazz of the period on tracks such as "Lullaby of Birdland", "S'Wonderful" and "Night & Day".

T H R E E

Saints & Sinners

Sister Rosetta Tharpe, Rev Gary Davis,
Josh White, Muddy Waters

L ike their black American predecessors including Mamie
Smith, Ma Rainey, Jimmy Rushing, and Joe Turner, the
first generation of British blues singers, notably George
Melly, Ottilie Patterson and Beryl Bryden sang with jazz bands
such as those of Mick Mulligan and Chris Barber. But during
the 1950s, British acoustic guitarists were also increasingly
influenced by guitarists/singers from black America, including on record, Leadbelly, who got to Paris but died in 1950
before he visited London, plus a number who were able to
visit – ignoring the union restrictions because they were solo
acts. They included Josh White who came to Britain first in
1950 when he was featured in a photograph on the front of
The Melody Maker with George Melly and Mick Mulligan, plus
Big Bill Broonzy (1951), Lonnie Johnson (1952), Sister Rosetta
Tharpe (1957), Brownie McGhee (with Sonny Terry, 1958),
Muddy Waters (1958) and Jesse Fuller (1959). They toured
mostly with British jazz bands and all returned at least once,
while other visitors in the 1950s included pianists Blind John
Davis (with Mahalia Jackson), Otis Spann (with Muddy Waters)
and Champion Jack Dupree, who eventually moved to Britain,
plus vocalist Brother John Sellers who like Josh White worked
across various styles and became involved in the New York folk
scene of the early 1960s.

Mahalia Jackson was one of the gospel's bigger stars, while another with an electric guitar and rock & roll 'edge', was Sister Rosetta Tharpe whose first visit to Portsmouth came in April 1960 with Chris Barber's Band. The *Evening News* described Tharpe being "at her exciting best" and the concert as "something no jazz lover should have missed", even praising Barber's band as "better than ever". They played the whole of the first half, then Sister Rosetta Tharpe opened the second with the band on "I Shall Not be Moved" before performing solo on "Moonshine", "Peace in the Valley", "Up Above My Head" and others, before the band returned for "The Saints" finale, after which she was "brought back for encore after encore until time ran out".

Bob Dawbarn of *The Melody Maker* reviewed Sister Rosetta Tharpe's 1960 show at the Royal Festival Hall, where she played a similar set, opening with "I Shall Not be Moved" accompanied by the band, then five songs just with her guitar: "This Train", "I Looked Down the Line", "Peace in the Valley", "Strange Things Happen Every Day" and "Motherless Children", before the band returned for "Up Above My Head", and three encores. Unlike Portsmouth, Ottilie Patterson sang with Tharpe on three songs, "When I Move to the Sky", "This Little Light of Mine" and "The Saints", and Dawbarn suggested this was to Patterson's advantage as she "sounded better when duetting … than on her own features". He praised Tharpe's "remarkable flexibility, breath control and impelling swing" – but he was exasperated by the audience who clapped along, with one exception, not "on the right beat"!

Another member of the 1964 Blues & Gospel Train was guitarist and singer the Reverend Gary Davis, a blind musician who came initially from Carolina on the east coast, before relocating to New York. Davis had a somewhat rough vocal delivery, somewhat like a Mississippi bluesman, but he was a sophisticated guitarist with a finger-picking style more typical of the players from the east coast including Brownie McGhee who was also on that 1964 tour. Davis was a big influence on Blind Boy Fuller, the most notable of the players from Carolina (the Piedmont scene) and both men played sometimes in ragtime, while Davis – ordained in the 1930s – sang more gospel songs than blues. Having recorded between the wars, Davis, along with such as Mississippi John Hurt, Sleepy John Estes, Skip James, and Son House was one of the older black musicians whose fortunes revived in the 1960s performing to a young mostly white, folk-oriented audience. While historically most blues records were recorded in the major cities such as Chicago, Memphis, or New York these acoustic musicians brought a rural feel which for some white 'disciples' added to the sense of 'authenticity'.

Gospel and other vocal forms including work songs and folk songs had their roots in spirituals, a somewhat old-fashioned term now but referring to a broad range of black American songs of the nineteenth century and before. On his British tour in 1956 Josh White was featured in a half-hour radio programme on the BBC's Home Service (now Radio Four) called "I Can Tell the World" (Friday 13 January) which *Radio Times* highlighted with an illustration of White playing and singing, and a caption reading "Negro Spirituals: at 8.0 Josh White sings songs in which the Negro expressed his faith". Josh White was accompanied in the programme by Jack Fallon on string bass, and a choir led by George Mitchell who a couple of years later would be responsible for assembling the *Black & White Minstrel Show* – as popular on British television and live shows as it was problematic, with its perpetuation of the blackface tradition. The producer of Josh White's programme, Charles Chilton, had previously presented his own jazz shows on BBC radio.

Rev. Gary Davis returned to the Guildhall in 1965, sharing a bill promoted by the English Folk Dance & Song Society with Native American Buffy Sainte Marie and Josh White. Post-war, some of the older black performers including Josh White might be referred to as 'folk' rather than 'blues' musicians; another was the somewhat idiosyncratic one-man band Jesse Fuller who toured Britain again in 1965, appearing on *Ready Steady Go!* where he performed his best-known song "San Francisco Bay Blues". During that tour he also played for a student 'folk' audience at Portsmouth's Clarence Pier, when the *Evening News* described him as "an authentic Negro folk singer" whose music "tends to be obscure".

It might be that the visits of Josh White and Brother John Sellers contributed in part to a brief period of popularity for Spirituals and African folk songs among white audiences. One or two songs taken up by white pop/folk acts even became hit records, including "Michael Row the Boat Ashore" a number one hit for the Highwaymen in September 1961 (and number six for Lonnie Donegan's version) and two differently-titled versions of the same song, "The Lion Sleeps Tonight" by the Tokens (number one, December 1961) and "Wimoweh" by Karl Denver (number four in the following month). In 1962 Joan Baez recorded a version of "Kumbaya" an African American spiritual which became associated with the Civil Rights movement, while three years later, her first single hit record in Britain was her version of "We Shall Overcome". In 1969 she sang "Swing Low Sweet Chariot" in her set at Woodstock – a song that from the late 1980s became the preferred song of England's rugby fans although recently its use in that context triggered a debate about its appropriateness. Other spirituals, some of which became staples of the Civil Rights movement and the growing folk scene, included "Go Down Moses (Let My People Go)", Rock My Soul (in the Bosom of Abraham)" – recorded by both Elvis Presley and Lonnie Donegan,

"This Little Light of Mine" and two slavery songs of escape: "Wade in the Water" and "Follow the Drinking Gourd".

The proliferation of spirituals and gospel songs through the 19th and 20th centuries reflected the extent to which many black Americans embraced Christianity and that included Christmas of course. Even in the seventeenth century slaves were permitted by their Christian masters to celebrate Christmas and Easter with a number of days 'holiday'. Music was always a part of those celebrations through the centuries and from the 1920s with the growing popularity of jazz and blues records many leading performers released records aimed at a Christmas market, including Bessie Smith, Victoria Spivey, Leroy Carr, Louis Armstrong, Fats Waller, Leadbelly, Joe Turner, Johnny Otis, Lionel Hampton, Louis Jordan, Ella Fitzgerald, Lightnin' Hopkins, Sonny Boy Williamson – even Charlie Parker with "White Christmas". This was a well-established tradition in popular music as the 1960s arrived, shared over 20 years by white performers like Bing Crosby, Frank Sinatra, Mel Tormé, Judy Garland, Andy Williams, Doris Day, and Elvis Presley, but in the 1960s, many in the new generation of 'swinging' sixties stars ignored the seasonal commercial opportunities, so there were no Christmas singles or albums from the likes of the Beatles, the Rolling Stones, the Bee Gees, Dusty Springfield, Bob Dylan, the Who, or the Kinks. It was a very different matter however with some of the leading black performers from that period with the Motown stars contributing to the label's Christmas albums, while the Ronettes, Crystals, Darlene Love and others were on the still very popular Phil Spector *Christmas Gift* album. There were other seasonal albums by Jackie Wilson, Huey 'Piano' Smith and singles from various doo-wop groups plus Otis Redding ("White Christmas" – also by the Drifters), Carla Thomas, Chuck Berry, the Dixie Cups, the Impressions, Percy Sledge, Solomon Burke and the Staple Singers.

By the time Josh White appeared at Portsmouth Guildhall, he was a polished performer who played in cabaret and the New York coffee house folk scene, although for some white audiences his 'sophistication' was not what they sought from black American performers although songs he and others recorded like "St James Infirmary" or "House of the Rising Sun" became staples of the early 1960s white folk scene on both sides of the Atlantic at a time when folk was flourishing among a new generation. Josh White also recorded familiar titles across a range of genres, including "Milk Cow Blues", "Stormy Weather", "Careless Love" and "Miss Otis Regrets", and in the 1940s he participated in the mixed-race Almanac Singers, a group that included at various times the white activist folk musicians Pete Seeger and Woody Guthrie. The variety of White's recorded output is not typical of black guitarist/singers but in 1965, he told Portsmouth's *Evening News* "my songs are still the people's songs. I still sing about the things that people can feel – all their happiness and all their grief".

In the mid-1950s, one manifestation of the influence of these visiting acoustic guitar players and American folk music more broadly which claimed very little in the way of sophistication came in the brief but highly significant British skiffle craze. Skiffle had its origins in the jazz clubs but burst into public prominence in Britain early in 1956 when (Tony) 'Lonnie' Donegan, the banjo player from the Chris Barber Jazz Band, entered the charts for the first time with a recording he had made originally as one of two 'skiffle' contributions to the band's new LP *New Orleans Joys*. The record company Decca had noted the popularity of the band's interval skiffle sessions, which featured Donegan on guitar and vocals with just Barber on double bass and washboard percussion, playing old American folk and blues songs many of which Donegan learned from records 'borrowed' from London's American Embassy. They were mostly simply three-chord arrangements in 4/4 time with basic backing and words and melodies that encouraged audiences to join in – "Rock Island Line" had a simple chorus for example – and after Donegan had enjoyed this first hit record, he went solo and launched the short-lived skiffle craze which nonetheless had repercussions beyond imagination for British popular music.

Skiffle was sufficiently simple that a 'D-I-Y' trend developed among teenagers, notably if not exclusively teenage boys, with skiffle groups and venues all springing up across the country. The groups generally featured acoustic guitars, washboards, and home-made 'tea-chest' one string bass instruments, and there are estimates that at the height of the craze there were at least 30,000 active groups in Britain. Some music shops struggled to keep up with the demand for acoustic guitars, while among the subsequent pop and rock stars who began their careers playing skiffle were members of the Shadows, Beatles and Rolling Stones, plus Van Morrison and schoolboy Jimmy Page who made an appearance playing guitar on BBC's children's television.

Given the number of skiffle groups around the country it was inevitable that Portsmouth would have its fair share and there are accounts in *the Evening News* of skiffle gigs and talent contests, with the local 'star' outfit probably that fronted by Mick Glover, a group that soon made the transition to rock & roll. After Glover went to the RAF on National Service the group renamed itself the Live Five and had a very brief spot in the early Cliff Richard film *Expresso Bongo*. In terms of this story however the one local skiffle group that really stands out for its subsequent influence on the spread and availability of black music in Britain emerged from Portsmouth Grammar School where a group of boys formed a skiffle group, called the

Louisiana Four: Christopher Bartle on banjo, David Rodgers on washboard, David Butlin on bass and David's best friend Paul Pond on guitar and vocals.

Butlin remembers that their group had a stronger 'blues' influence than other local skiffle groups through the influence of Paul Pond – Butlin recalls that while his friends were keen to play the latest Elvis hit record, Paul would insist on playing King Oliver's "Dippermouth Blues". From this classic 1920s New Orleans jazz recording it was a relatively short distance to the blues such as was available in Britain in the mid-1950s – mostly from specialist shops like *Dobell's* in Charing Cross Road. Paul would make the trip to the shops and clubs in London where perhaps he encountered live performances by Alexis Korner, Cyril Davies, George Melly, Ottilie Patterson and others, as the blues first surfaced in this country. After a short stay at Oxford University, Paul Pond began pursuing a career as a singer, teaming-up briefly with Brian Jones prior to his being a founder member of the Rolling Stones. Paul eventually joined up with drummer Mike Hugg from Gosport and pianist Manfred Mann as they shifted from a modern jazz sound towards the newly fashionable British R&B. Paul Pond changed his surname to Jones and for decades has been a leading figure on the British blues scene, partly as vocalist and harmonica player in the long-running Blues Band but also for many years presenting regular blues radio shows on BBC's Radio Two and Jazz FM.

One of the 'new' guitarists, Chas McDevitt, like Donegan, an experienced banjo player, had visited Southsea's Savoy Ballroom a number of times in the 1950s with his traditional jazz band the High Curley Stompers. He saw the possibilities for commercial success in skiffle, persuaded Scottish folk singer Nancy Whiskey to join a new group and their recording of "Freight

Train" reached the Top Ten in April 1957. The song wrongly attributed initially to two British songwriters was finally and correctly identified with an American black woman, the singer and guitarist Elizabeth Cotton, who worked for the musical Seeger family. Like "Rock Island Line" and other American folk and blues songs, it became a staple of many British skiffle groups in the second half of the 1950s. By the time Lonnie Donegan appeared at the King's Theatre in February 1960, he was billed with a "Full West End Company" having moved towards the status of 'all-round entertainer' with a set that included "Mr Froggy Went A-Courting", "Miss Otis Regrets", "Gambling Man", Battle of New Orleans" and comedy numbers. The *Evening News* reported "the skiffle king still reigns supreme", with the second house sold out, and there was "noise from teenage girls in the balcony".

While Lonnie pursued a mass audience, many young skiffle guitarists switched to electric guitars and the world of pop and rock, while others became adept at the acoustic guitar and would feature strongly on the British folk scene of the 1960s. On Thursday 16 June, 1960, at the Star in Lake Road, local jazz fan and trumpeter Ted Laker "tried the 'Ballads and Blues' club", another new venture by Frank Hurlock where he heard what he called "some goodish folk music". While this was somewhat lukewarm praise, he continued to attend and at a session in August 1960 wrote positively about hearing "some good Josh White records", a few years before White's Portsmouth performance.

In January 1963, the *Evening News* launched a new series, 'Off Beat', "covering all fields of jazz", and on its debut to its main features on Duke Ellington and Dave Brubeck's saxophonist Paul Desmond the 'Jazzmen' authors added a third piece suggesting "skiffle is back" in the "disguise" of the local folk clubs. To emphasise the skiffle link, the piece mentioned "American folk", reporting on two clubs in the Fratton area that offered, "an amazingly wide range of the styles grouped under this general heading" of folk.

If there was a link between jazz and the increasingly popular folk music in post-war Britain it was perhaps less about what was played and heard and more about a rejection of more 'mainstream' entertainment, whether that was the perceived elitism of the classical world or the somewhat predictable output of the familiar dance bands and smooth, easy-listening sounds of the newly- founded 'Hit Parade'. When that was first published in Britain by the *New Musical Express* in November 1952, American crooner Al Martino was at number one with "Here in My Heart" and the other acts featured were almost all solo singers from the USA including Jo Stafford, Bing Crosby, Rosemary Clooney, Frankie Laine, Doris Day and Johnny Ray, along with British singers Max Bygraves and Vera Lynn. Nat King Cole, at number three with "Somewhere Along the Way" was the one black performer although pianist Winifred Atwell from Trinidad but British-based, brought instrumental piano ragtime into the charts briefly in mid-December and over the Christmas holidays of 1953 & 1954 her "party" records were very popular; she was the first black person to have a number-one hit in the British charts – and is still the only one having done so with an instrumental.

Jazz, folk and their offshoots, blues and skiffle, were by contrast perceived as more 'authentic', more rooted in the real lives of ordinary people while offering also a certain sometimes danger-ous exoticism in the music and culture of 'other' peoples. This in turn sometimes linked to a left-of-centre politics during a period of growing commitment to issues around the Suez crisis (1956) or the nuclear threat and the growth of CND, with

Black, White and the Blues

the latter's marches between London and Aldermaston always accompanied by folk guitarists and revivalist jazz bands. In addition, while classical orchestras and dance bands employed accomplished professional musicians, skiffle, folk and some ensemble New Orleans-style jazz provided performing opportunities for the committed amateur.

Lonnie Donegan was the man who brought skiffle into popular entertainment in Britain, but the first significant British skiffle recordings were made by jazz trumpeter Ken Colyer and he took a very different approach. Colyer was a fierce advocate of an 'authentic' approach to the performance of New Orleans jazz and the blues element of early skiffle prior to its commercialisation. Like Colyer, Ewan MacColl and his partner, American Peggy Seeger the key figures on the burgeoning folk scene, held strict views about what was and was not acceptable and declared a strict policy for their Ballads and Blues Club, which was adopted by a few other clubs that followed the 'rules' and featured mostly unaccompanied singers or traditional instruments like fiddle or concertina.

That dictatorial approach did not always help attendances in the clubs nationwide, but there was another, eclectic attitude, more typical of the Portsmouth folk scene, and far more dependent on the guitar as its principal instrument. The guitarists were often open to a range of influences, including blues and ragtime by black American performers and the main British guitarists included Davey Graham perhaps the most wide-ranging and experimental of them all, plus others like Al Stewart, Ralph McTell, and Bert Jansch, all of whom played in Portsmouth's folk clubs. A major event was the visit to the Railway Folk Club of the blind white American guitarist and singer Doc Watson who offered a range of folk, blues and bluegrass songs and a mastery of the flat-picking and finger-picking acoustic guitar styles.

As with the post-war jazz scene, the way that most of these performers drew upon and sometimes performed covers of the older generation of black American guitarists and singers was one key element of the folk revival. One regular visitor to Portsmouth's folk clubs was the Indian-born, London-based guitarist and singer Gerry Lockran whose style owed much to later solo recordings by Big Bill Broonzy, and other white guitarists and singers who played mainly blues and related repertoires in British clubs, included Long John Baldry, Jo Ann Kelly, Mike Cooper and American Stephane Grossman all of whom appeared in Portsmouth. There were also a few black folk artists on the circuit who came to the city including British-based Californian-raised Dorris Henderson (later of Eclection) Nadia Cattouse from Belize who enjoyed a sell-out night at the Folkhouse Club, and Johnny Silvo who made an LP *Sandy & Johnny*, sharing tracks with Sandy Denny which were her first recordings. As folk grew in popularity there were concerts at the Oddfellows Hall, the Guildhall and as the 1960s drew to a close, the King's Theatre which presented an acoustic night entitled "Folk Blues & Beyond", starring Al Stewart, Ralph McTell, Michael Chapman, Diz Disley, Wizz Jones and local guitarist/singer Pete Quinn.

But there was another post-war blues guitar style in the USA which ultimately had a bigger impact on British music. It came mainly out of Chicago, with its roots in Mississippi, in some cases like Muddy Waters and Elmore James made greater use of the slide or bottleneck on the left-hand, and eventually was enhanced more generally through greatly improved amplification.

While Muddy Waters and his 1950s band were major exponents of the 'electric' blues style, he was initially recorded acoustically in the summers of 1941 and 1942 and his recording history offers one of the clearest examples of the shift from rural acoustic or string band styles to urban ensemble electric blues. Muddy Waters (1915-1983) was born and raised in Mississippi and at the time of those earliest recordings was working on Stovall's Plantation, Mississippi. By 1964 he was a long-established leading figure in Chicago and throughout the USA, and his music was becoming well-known in Britain partly through LP records and also covers of his songs by the new British R&B groups such as the Rolling Stones (named after one of Muddy Waters' songs), Alexis Korner's Blues Incorporated, the Yardbirds, Manfred Mann and others. There was always a debate about whether these white, initially British, groups were exploiting their acknowledged masters but years later (April 1977) in a lengthy interview in *NME,* Muddy Waters told Charles Shaar Murray

> It was the Beatles and Rolling Stones. The Beatles did a lot of Chuck Berry, the Rolling Stones did some of my stuff. That's what it took to wake up the people in my own country, in my own state where I was born, that a black man's music is not a crime to bring into the house.

The first recording sessions with Muddy Waters and others by Alan Lomax were not initially for commercial release, they were made for the USA's Library of Congress and included various spoken interviews, plus Muddy and his guitar singing "Country Blues", "I Be's Troubled" and "Burr Clover Farm Blues". The latter track included a second guitarist Son Simms who also led his own quartet, playing violin, and included Waters plus Percy Thomas (guitar) and Louis Ford (mandolin). In the second session for Lomax they recorded four tracks playing as a typical black string band reminiscent of even earlier days, to which Muddy Waters added four more songs with either Simms or Charles Berry on second guitar. These tracks were released commercially in Britain in 1966, as *Down on Stovall's Plantation* and while through his career Muddy Waters was very much a secular blues singer, the first recordings included Muddy and his slide guitar performing "Why Don't You Live So God Can Use You". The album was reviewed by editor Bob Groom in his British-based modestly-produced magazine *Blues World* in September 1966 where he described "the musical riches" in "this wonderful compilation", adding praise for "Muddy, the Country-Bluesman displaying sensitive, subtle guitar-playing and a moving vocal style".

Almost all black American music whether it was live, on radio or on record that is now available for us to hear was produced or made available for commercial purposes – even eventually these recordings by Muddy Waters, following that mid-1960s commercial release. As a consequence, hardly any of it replicated *directly* the centuries-old vernacular music of slavery or the *post-bellum* years of so-called emancipation. Apart from the comparatively few 'documentary' recordings by John & Alan Lomax and others, most of what we heard and hear in Britain dates from the release of commercial recordings starting around the end of the First World War and it is through those recordings from the past by commercial record companies that most history and most judgements emerge.

In 1943, like many other black Americans, Muddy Waters left Mississippi and moved north to Chicago, where he found employment and continued to perform. Three years later he began recording, and a key moment in his long career came in 1948 when he recorded his first blues using electric guitar, for the Aristocrat label. The label was established by the Polish Chess brothers, Leonard and Phil, who soon changed its name to Chess and by the mid-1950s Muddy Waters' records like "Hoochie, Coochie Man", "I'm Ready" and "Mannish Boy" were making the American R&B charts.

Despite the mid-1950s challenge of rock & roll, he was fairly settled in his Chicago career but in 1958 he accepted an invitation to tour Britain with the Chris Barber Band, who had already toured with black American acts including the gospel singer Sister Rosetta Tharpe, the folk-blues duo Sonny Terry & Brownie McGhee and the Modern Jazz Quartet. When Muddy Waters came to Britain with his pianist and half-brother Otis Spann they played with Barber's rhythm section occasionally to a somewhat mixed reception, as British blues fans learned about contemporary black American music. Having become familiar with the jazz-oriented 'Classic' women singers of the 1920s, such as Ma Rainey or Bessie Smith, and the acoustic folk-blues guitarists like Leadbelly – filtered through the skiffle boom of 1956/7 – plus recent visitors Big Bill Broonzy and Brownie McGhee, they were apparently unprepared for Muddy Waters performing with a solid-bodied Fender Telecaster and amplifier – the early headlines warned of "Screaming Guitar and Howling Piano".

As a consequence, in 1963, when Muddy Waters returned to tour Britain with one of the first American blues 'package' tours, he came with an acoustic guitar – or sometimes just as a singer. By this time however, a younger generation of blues fans, many coming to the blues through rock & roll, skiffle and early British R&B, were anticipating the Muddy Waters of the amplified Chicago club scene, playing tracks that were familiar through albums released in Britain on the Pye label. This time, it was their turn to be disappointed – they wanted to hear him amplified in a Chicago-style band. There is a stylish but restrained video recording of Muddy on that tour singing "Got My Mojo Working" with a band including Willie Dixon on string bass, Otis Spann on piano and Sonny Boy Williamson on harmonica – but no "screaming" guitar.

That tour, called the 'American Negro Blues Festival', covered Europe including two shows (6.30 & 8.50 pm) at the Fairfield Hall Croydon and an album was released featuring the various acts including those mentioned above and two veterans' of the 1920s, guitarist Lonnie Johnson and singer Victoria Spivey, plus pianist Memphis Slim, Mississippi Delta guitarist and singer Big Joe Williams (1902-1983), best known for his version of "Baby Please Don't Go", and Matt 'Guitar' Murphy. In September 1963, perhaps responding to the growing fashion for acoustic folk-blues among young white audiences on both sides of the Atlantic, Muddy Waters recorded his fourth studio album: *Muddy Waters Folk Singer*. The album features Waters on acoustic guitar (including slide), backed by Willie Dixon on string bass, Clifton James on drums, and Buddy Guy on acoustic guitar. It is Waters' only all-acoustic album and very restrained in comparison with his mid/late-1950s recordings or the covers of those songs by British R&B groups.

In 1964, just as that album was being released, Muddy Waters returned to Britain for the third time and on this occasion he came to Portsmouth Guildhall where in April 1964 the *Evening News* reported a "heavy demand" for tickets. This 'package' tour was the American Folk Blues and Gospel Caravan and as well as the previously mentioned, Rev Gary Davis, Sister Rosetta Tharpe, Brownie McGhee (with Sonny Terry) and Muddy Waters there was Muddy's pianist Otis Spann his bass player Ransom Knowling, and drummer Willie Smith plus the New Orleans pianist Cousin Joe Pleasants. The show was reviewed in *the Evening News* by JN who suggested "it was one of the most swinging romps Portsmouth has seen", adding oddly that "the blues, sad and wailing were not in evidence". This view is somewhat contradicted by other accounts of Muddy Waters' performance at least but JN suggested "it was happiness all the way", perhaps because of the presence of two gospel singers and also the typical humour of New Orleans pianist Cousin Joe Pleasants who was "the most popular". Otherwise JN saw Sonny Terry & Brownie McGhee" as the "nearest to what was expected from a folksy evening", while Sister Rosetta Tharpe "brought emotion to the stage" despite her religious lyrics "clashing strangely with snappy guitar" and "pop star" movements. Rev. Gary Davis was "perhaps the most authentic" and Muddy Waters catered for "the rhythm & blues fans" playing blues "for dancing and foot-tapping". Overall, he felt it was a "joyful" evening.

One week after the Portsmouth date, Granada Television broadcast a show of the tour (including Southern Television) from a disused railway station near Manchester, where on a stormy night Muddy Waters performed "Blow Wind, Blow", and Sister Rosetta Tharpe regaled the clapping audience with "Didn't It Rain?". The bill was varied with Muddy Waters and Otis Spann representing the increasing popular and contemporary style of Chicago blues, but Waters' performance in Portsmouth had troubled an *Evening News* correspondent Brian Chalker, described as a "local expert on folk music". He praised the show overall but was critical of Muddy Waters for being "monotonous", with the first four "slow" songs ("dancing and foot-tapping"?) in the same key, after which he was "reprieved" by a familiar version of "Got My Mojo Working" before he "sank back again". Chalker considered his performance a "big disappointment", although attempting to balance his criticism with the surprising observation that Muddy Waters' guitar playing "was extremely pleasant". A few weeks later Chalker was in print again, complaining about the "indiscriminate use of the word folk to describe any variety of singers" – and once again he picked on Muddy Waters who he felt did not qualify. He defined folk as "the music of the people for the people by the people – and a folk song has no known author". During the same year he offered evaluations of singers

Jim Reeves and Roger Miller in a piece in which *the Evening News* described him knowing "as much about country & western as anyone in Britain".

Almost sixty years later we have no record of Muddy Waters' performance in Portsmouth and it is difficult to be clear about exactly where Mr Chalker stood more broadly – it is after all no simple thing to be an expert on all the various forms of folk, blues and country music – but we do have a recording of Muddy Waters from the television programme of the same tour from which anyone familiar with his music in the mid-1960s would surely recognise it as a typically rich performance by one of the major blues musicians of the century. In retrospect Brian Chalker's criticism is perhaps indicative of a predominant view locally – maybe across Britain – of the black music and musicians we encountered in this post-war period. For perhaps 20 years after the war, many committed British fans of jazz, blues and other black styles preferred to look back towards the jazz of New Orleans, the acoustic blues guitarists or 1920s 'Classic' women singers, the big bands of the 1930s and 1940s or the fine singing of Ella Fitzgerald, Sarah Vaughan and others – they often seemed less fond of contemporary developments in black American music. But an interesting change occurred initially and briefly with fans of black rock & roll singers and then more significantly from the mid-1960s when a new generation discovered and enjoyed contemporary electric blues and modern soul, ska and reggae. Suddenly, these younger fans were not looking back but enjoying the present although even that shift towards contemporary black music was not across the board – it would be difficult to argue for example, that there was a big following for the increasingly 'free-form' jazz of Ornette Coleman, Albert Ayler and others. From the mid-1960s however, visiting black musicians appearing in Portsmouth were increasingly contemporary, popular, and performing mostly to a new 'sixties' audience.

Folk music or not, as the blues became increasingly popular in Britain in their own right as opposed to being an adjunct of jazz the Folk Blues and Gospel Caravan was one of a number of such tours, starting with the first of a succession of American Folk Blues Festivals which came to Europe in 1962; usually followed by a live album. The particular package that came to Portsmouth offered a glimpse of a broad range of black American styles, a real education for British fans, so that anyone in the almost wholly white provincial audience at the Guildhall would have gone away with an enhanced idea of the sounds of ragtime, modern gospel, New Orleans piano, folk-blues and the modern Chicago amplified ensemble – confirmed by the television broadcast that followed. Through the 1960s and beyond, black American blues would become a growing and significant influence on British popular music.

F O U R

Good Rockin' Tonight

Louis Jordan, Little Richard, Ray Charles, Nina Simone

The Post-war Chicago blues bands mostly featured amplified guitars, harmonicas and sometimes piano, whereas elsewhere, rhythm & blues groups of around six or seven members might still feature more familiar front-line jazz instruments for example Louis Jordan's Tympani Five in which Jordan sang and played saxophone with trumpet, piano and string bass. Later in his life Jordan revealed that while he had loved playing the blues and big band jazz (notably with Chick Webb) he "really wanted to be an entertainer" and "play for the people". In this, with an economically manageable smaller band he followed the example of a performer like Cab Calloway and enjoyed regular post-war hits on the R&B charts, playing a significant part in the development of rhythm & blues and rock & roll. Some years after his major successes, in December 1962, he appeared at the Guildhall, without the Tympani Five but with Chris Barber's Jazz Band.

British jazz critic Peter Clayton wrote programme notes for that British tour, revealing that only a few weeks earlier Chris Barber had discovered Jordan still performing in America and in his typically pioneering way persuaded him to join them on this British tour. Clayton described how he had first encountered Jordan's then fairly unfamiliar music in a movie clip of American musicians entertaining their troops in the Second World War when "Jordan, the leader, was a vigorous and exhilarating performer who sang with colossal gusto and occasionally played stabbing and uncomplicated choruses on alto saxophone". Clayton wondered whether "we had a name for it in England at that time, but this was, I suppose, our first taste of what we shouldn't hesitate now to call a rhythm and blues band" although he added "the noise they made was superior to the honest but raw endeavours of most of the R & B electricians' groups at present roaring about on the London scene".

Since this was in late 1962 Alexis Korner's Blues Incorporated were perhaps the only notable British blues band playing, broadcasting and recording around London; an early version of the Rolling Stones was still some months away from their first recordings while in the provinces British jazz still held sway over anything very close to electric R&B. Clayton also suspected that in 1962 there were hardly any Louis Jordan records available in Britain, unlike today when even his old 'soundie' short films are freely available on You Tube, so, he suggested "for most people Jordan is going to be something of a discovery ... while his style has probably changed very little over the past 25 years ... (he) ... will almost certainly sound 'new' and exciting to British audiences".

Milt Gabler, Jordan's 1940s record producer, later worked on the early hit records by Bill Haley & his Comets, and Jordan was described by the American Rock & Roll Hall of Fame as "The Father of Rhythm & Blues" and "The Grandfather of Rock 'n' Roll". He was a fine performer with amusing songs like "Ain't Nobody Here but Us Chickens", or "What's the Use of Getting Sober" to which he added hit records such as "Caldonia", "Choo Choo Ch' Boogie" and "Let the Good Times Roll". In the 1990s the hit musical "Five Guys Named Moe" was based on one of those film 'shorts' of the 1940s, featured many of the Tympani Five's songs and ran successfully in London's West End, Europe and on Broadway. Then in 1999, BB King, backed by members of Ray Charles' band, recorded a tribute album *Let the Good Times Roll: The Music of Louis Jordan*; Ray Charles was one of two black American artists particularly influenced by Louis Jordan who would visit Portsmouth in the 1960s – the other was Little Richard.

Little Richard came to Portsmouth in November 1966, ten years after he had first appeared in the British top thirty with "Rip It Up", after which, in February 1957, he reached number three with "Long Tall Sally" – an early feature in the Beatles set, and the title track of their fifth EP. Little Richard was perhaps the 'wildest' of the early rock & rollers, toning down the original gay sex lyrics of his third British hit, "Tutti Frutti" with its immortal opening line "Awop Bop Aloo Bop Alop Bam Boom". In 2007, *Mojo* magazine placed it at number one in their feature, "The Top 100 Records That Changed the World" and the Beatles also covered that song but while their guitar-based line-up echoed many early mostly white, rock & rollers like Bill Haley, Elvis, Chuck Berry, Carl Perkins, Eddie Cochran and Buddy Holly, who sang and played guitar, Little Richard was a pianist with a band that featured saxophones – more obviously in the style of the post-war black rhythm & blues bands, including Louis Jordan's. Little Richard's live performance can be seen to good effect in the film *The Girl Can't Help It* in which he sang the title track and that recording reached the British top ten in March 1957. "Good Golly Miss Molly" and "Baby Face" were other top ten British hits in the late 1950s but then for a brief period he turned his back on these songs and extravagant performances, becoming a preacher, which musically at least fitted with his gospel roots. He returned to rock & roll music in the 1960s and gave a thrilling, memorable performance in Portsmouth's crowded Birdcage Club where the usual mod audience was pushed to the edges by the local Teddy Boys who crowded to the front of the stage.

Teddy Boys predated the arrival of rock & roll in Britain but they adopted it as their own, as a succession of new black and white American artists followed Bill Haley & his Comets into the British charts for the first time. This began in May 1956 with Elvis Presley's "Heartbreak Hotel", followed by Carl Perkins ("Blue Suede Shoes"), Frankie Lymon & the Teenagers ("Why Do Fools Fall in Love"), Gene Vincent ("Be-Bop-A-Lula), Fats Domino ("I'm in Love Again"), and Clyde McPhatter ("Treasure of Love"). By late September Elvis with "Hound Dog" and Bill Haley ("Razzle Dazzle") were back in the charts followed by Little Richard ("Rip It Up") before Christmas, although "Long Tall Sally" had already been in the charts courtesy of an anodyne cover by Pat Boone. Boone was not the only white performer with little feel for rock & roll to exploit the commercial possibilities of the new sound as Britain's Alma Cogan released her version of "Why Do Fools Fall in Love", and there were a couple of 'comic' efforts from the Goons ("Bloodnok's Rock & Roll Call") and Stan Freiberg's "Heartbreak Hotel" b/w "Rock Island Line" which appeared in the Top Thirty. The biggest 'exploitation' hit though was Kay Starr's "Rock & Roll Waltz" which reached number one in March 1956. Despite its success, as a waltz in 3/4 time it ignored entirely the importance of the 'backbeat' in almost all up-tempo rhythm & blues and rock & roll of the 1940s, 1950s.

The impact of rock & roll and the creation of an audience for it in Britain raised the possibilities of British outfits emulating their predecessors in traditional and modern jazz, dance bands and skiffle. Could Britain find its own rock & roll live acts to meet the demands of this new audience, especially as these American performers would not tour regularly and some, not least Elvis Presley, not at all? It would not be long before local skiffle groups, bought amplifiers and drum kits and learned the latest songs, in Portsmouth the Cadillacs, attired in fine red drape suits were an early example, but might there be more?

The answer came in the form of a British modern jazz and big band drummer who had appeared in Portsmouth on a number of occasions in recent years. Tony Crombie, a colleague of Ronnie Scott in Club Eleven in the 1940s saw an opportunity to break away from the financial uncertainty of his professional life by assembling Britain's first professional, touring and recording rock & roll group. There was a precedent in Crombie's case; in January 1954 *The Melody* Maker reported he was assembling "what is claimed to be Britain's first rhythm and blues band", including fellow modern jazz musicians Joe Harriott and Benny Green and "guest appearances" from Ronnie Scott and Art Baxter. Oddly no vocalist was identified and little more was heard of the band that had made their debut at the Flamingo but in 1956, he created this new group and taking a lead from Bill Haley & his Comets named it Tony Crombie & the Rockets. Their launch in September 1956 had interesting, indeed historic implications for popular music in Portsmouth.

On Sunday 9 September 1956, Elvis Presley made his first appearance on the American national television broadcast of the Ed Sullivan Show. On the following day, the Portsmouth *Evening News* published a letter condemning outbreaks of violence in cinemas showing the latest rock & roll movies in which AB Conning (*sic*) described "crack-brained teenagers capering in the aisles" and condemned the "disgracefully low" fines on those who misbehaved. The Portsmouth cinemas that week were more restrained, showing recent celluloid endeavours by Lana Turner, Bob Hope, Tony Curtis and Richard Burton but there was excitement of the new kind at the Theatre Royal that Monday evening.

The new weekly show was typical of the 1950s variety bill that the ailing theatre hoped would keep it operational. The programme listed an opening at 6.20 pm with an overture by the orchestra, followed by dancers Nick & Pat Lundon, comedian Johnny Dallas and singers, Billie Wyner, Maxine Daniels, the "coloured singing star of television and Oriole Records", and "dynamic" Don Fox. After the interval the dancers returned, then Scottish TV "funster" Andy Stewart and mime artists Ross & Howitt. So far this was pretty normal fare but to finish, Bernard Delfont presented the live debut of the new six-piece British "Rock 'n' Roll" act, Tony Crombie and his Rockets.

In the following week, the group were booked into the prestigious London Palladium, followed by a national tour, so the decision had been taken to give them a week in the provinces to hone their act and Portsmouth was chosen for the 'birth' of British rock & roll. The Rockets then recorded and released the first British rock & roll record "Teach You to Rock" the title tune from a British movie in which they appeared and it entered the British charts in mid-October 1956. Over the next 50 years, the city of Portsmouth might warrant little more than a footnote in the history of British popular music but on this night it was centre stage at the 'birth' of British rock & roll.

In the following day's review, *the Evening News* suggested that the saxophone had been under-amplified but was otherwise enthusiastic. The main headline "Rock 'n' Roll Greeted with Cheers" preceded a generally positive review of "the most controversial music craze since the Charleston". The review reported this was "no wild, riotous debut" to cause anxiety but rather a performance ending "with cheering and applause that rocked the theatre". The teenage audience were "shirt-sleeved and sweatered" – fashion and image already linked inextricably to the new sounds in popular music. The newspaper suggested this youthful enthusiasm might be considered "mass hysteria, exhibitionism or plain audience participation", suggesting "Rock 'n' Roll may die soon" although "at the moment it is a lusty, rowdy, healthy infant". Of course it was the live variety circuit that effectively died away while rock & roll grew into a fully-fledged, affluent and sometimes naughty adult.

Rock & roll and skiffle may have sounded like a dramatic change from what had gone before but 'skiffle king' Lonnie Donegan had emerged as a banjo player from the already popular traditional jazz scene while Tony Crombie had spent more than a decade playing in dance bands and modern jazz groups. They were not from the new generation and like Bill Haley they looked pretty conventional. In a matter of years Donegan was pursuing the path of a comic and all-round enter- tainer, while it was his disciples including the Beatles, Rolling Stones, Van Morrison and Jimmy Page who forged the new paths. Tony Crombie's Rockets soon slipped out of the charts, never to return, deposed by the first big star of British rock & roll Tommy Steele whose "Rock with the Caveman" was just a week behind Crombie – and by Christmas, Steele was at number one with his follow-up, "Singing the Blues". Tony Crombie meanwhile soon re-assembled his Orchestra and was back at the Savoy entertaining the dancers.

While skiffle and early rock & roll grew from older musical styles on both sides of the Atlantic, there were also essential differences and clear breaks with the past, which would lead to the dramatic innovations of the following decade. One differ- ence was a younger audience for this new music, teenagers and young adults who were enjoying an unprecedented level of economic independence, and this explains in part why the somewhat staid, imitative Rockets were ousted by the raw teenage star Tommy Steele complete with cockney accent and crew-cut. Tommy of course soon departed that teenage scene, following Donegan to pursue a successful career as an all-round entertainer, and briefly the British rock & roll mantle was passed to Cliff Richard ("Move It"), Marty Wilde, Billy Fury and perhaps the rawest, most dynamic act Johnny Kidd & the Pirates. But British rock & roll was always second best to the original American version – especially as 1956 drew to a close, with Chuck Berry, Jerry Lee Lewis, Eddie Cochran and Buddy Holly following the first hit parade pioneers.

To a considerable extent the new music had its roots in black rhythm and blues vocal traditions, which, as Peter Clayton suggested, were then unfamiliar to most British audiences and musicians. By the time the next generation spearheaded the beat and R&B 'revolution' in 1963 those musicians were better acquainted with blues, rhythm & blues and rock & roll. For the first time too, British popular music was guitar-based with the historic problems of audibility solved by the proliferation of intimate venues, especially coffee bars, and the development of more powerful pick-ups and amplifiers for larger venues. The other impact of the guitar and of skiffle was in the emerging folk scene, where the guitars remained acoustic.

During the 1950s the smaller seven-inch, 45 rpm singles were replacing the old, larger 78 rpm format, for example the last hit single by Elvis Presley released on 78 rpm in Britain was "Mess of Blues" in the summer of 1960, by which time it would have also been available on the smaller format, the one that led to the proliferation of juke boxes in the coffee bars frequented by teenagers. In Portsmouth there was also Billy Manning's seafront funfair where the Waltzer in particular played the latest hit records pretty much non-stop, while the many youth clubs soon provided record players for their members to play the new records.

In Portsmouth in the late-1950s, promoter Reg Calvert staged rock & roll dances at the Oddfellows Hall in Kingston Road with popular British stars, and there were also singing contests with the likelihood that one of the local Teddy Boys would 'attract' most support (or else) in an early Pompey version of *The X Factor*. There were occasional nights for rock & roll at venues like Ricky's in Goldsmith Avenue or Caesar's Club in North End, while the Court Dancing School in Eastney began featuring live rock & roll groups on Saturday nights, including the Hot Rods and Danny Raven & the Renegades. At the Guildhall, Jerry Lee Lewis, headed a bill in 1962 that included Johnny Kidd & the Pirates, and Vince Eagar while at Easter of the same year three Americans Johnny Burnette, and two black singers Gary US Bonds ("New Orleans") and Gene McDaniels ("Tower of Strength") joined Mark Wynter at the Guildhall.

A major black American star who certainly 'rocked & rolled' while incorporating a broader range of styles, often rooted in gospel and rhythm & blues was the blind pianist and singer Ray Charles (1932-2004) who appeared at the Guildhall in 1964. Ray Charles like Little Richard, was born in Macon Georgia and through his long and productive career he covered many styles including blues, gospel – with a highly effective use of call & response – modern jazz, rock & roll and, to notable effect, country & western, a reminder that in the southern states, blues, folk and country styles had always been exchanged between black and white performers. Rock & roll is generally seen as bringing together rhythm & blues, country/hillbilly and western swing and in the case of someone like Little Richard, gospel.

Bill Haley for example recorded in the 1940s with his band the Four Aces of Western Swing and then the Saddlemen, while early in his years fronting the Comets he enjoyed a rock & roll hit with a sanitised cover of Big Joe Turner's "Shake Rattle & Roll". Similarly, "My Baby Left Me", the first single Elvis Presley recorded for the Sun label in 1954 was a cover of a 1940s recording by blues singer Arthur 'Big Boy' Crudup, while on the 'B' side was an up-tempo version of Bill Monroe's bluegrass song "Blue Moon of Kentucky", and in 1956, Chuck Berry's first single release "Maybellene" was a reworking of the country song "Ida Red". There are many other examples of this cross-fertilisation, going back to the earliest recordings of blues, country, string band and jug band musicians of the 1920s.

In the USA, Ray Charles enjoyed an R&B chart career across seven decades, while in Britain his chart success began around Christmas 1960 when his version of Hoagy Carmichael's "Georgia on my Mind" reached the top thirty. Ten months later, "Hit the Road Jack" made the top ten, then in the summer of 1962 came the first of two volumes of his albums *Modern Sounds in Country and Western Music,* which reached the British top ten in the album charts, while a single from that LP, "I Can't Stop Loving You" reached number one. Further top twenty hits followed from these crossover albums: "You Don't Know Me", "Your Cheating Heart" and "Take These Chains from My Heart".

Ray Charles appeared at the Guildhall in July 1964 with his Orchestra during a somewhat difficult tour, partly complicated as it coincided with Ray Charles' part in the film *Ballad in Blue,* with shooting scheduled for London, Paris and Dublin. The orchestra consisted of 13 men on brass and reeds, plus guitar, bass and drums, with Charles on piano and as usual the instruments were intended to be enhanced by the four-piece female chorus, the Raelets including their leader Margie Hendricks although they failed to appear early on in the tour, indisposed according to the *NME* as a result of the English climate. Apparently there was a conflict between Charles and Hendricks which ended their personal relationship and the absence of the fully-functioning quartet was reported to impact adversely on the performances, although the review in *the Evening News* described a quartet of un-named singers, but with a disappointing "pre-war sound". The reviewer (SR) also found the first half, featuring the Orchestra without the star less than satisfactory, as they produced a "woolly" sound despite "far from demanding scores".

But whatever the difficulties of the tour overall, or the first half in Portsmouth, SR was in no doubt of the quality of Ray Charles through the second half. The headline "Charles Jazz and Pop Star" led to a description of his accomplished moving between genres and styles, suggesting when he is "in town, all boundaries are down. He is the jazz singer, the blues pianist with a pop programme" handling the blues "superbly". SR described a fine version of "Making Whoopee" and doubted whether "an artist lives who could better his performance of "In the Evening" or "That Lucky Old Sun"". We have no complete account of his set list for the Portsmouth gig, but from another unnamed night on the tour, an audio recording reveals others including "You Don't Know Me", "Just a Little Lovin'", "Georgia on my Mind", "Careless Love", "Hallelujah I Love Her So", "Born to Lose", I've Got a Woman", and "Busted".

This ability to work across styles and genres, creating a highly personal sound might be seen as entirely positive but there were a number of comments and letters in the *Evening News* about the visit of Ray Charles, some of which indicated debates at that time around concepts like authenticity and 'purity'. One correspondent suggested his music had "as much relationship to jazz as Elvis Presley's" dismissing him as "a purely commercial artist", although another writer was tired of "small-minded" views and praised his use of "improvisation" and his "experimental" approach. One of his concerts on the tour, in Croydon, was recorded for British television and shown as a 45-minute feature in August although sadly the footage did not survive.

Ray Charles was a big influence on the British beat and R&B groups of the early 1960s – the Beatles included "What'd I Say" in their unsuccessful audition for Decca Records in 1962, while perhaps the particular group to draw on his songs were the Animals, vocalist Eric Burdon was a big fan and they recorded versions of Ray Charles records, "The Night Time is the Right Time", "Mess Around", "Hallelujah I Love Her So" and "I Believe to my Soul". The Spencer Davis Group included Ray Charles' version of "Georgia on my Mind" on their second album, while in the 1960s the big band rhythm & blues of the Ray Charles Orchestra also influenced the British jazz-oriented R&B bands like Georgie Flame & the Blue Flames and Zoot Money's Big Roll Band – the latter included "Smack Dab in the Middle" and "Hallelujah I Love Her So" in their live performances. Meanwhile, emulating the fuller sound of the Ray Charles Orchestra at the Richmond Jazz & Blues Festival in 1965, the Animals added a seven-piece brass/reeds section, and in the following year Georgie Fame & the Blue Flames teamed up with the Harry South Big Band to record the album *Sound Venture.*

Ray Charles had worked as pianist in the 1940s rhythm & blues band of West Coast guitarist and blues singer Lowell Fulson and that experience was evident in the sound of his Orchestra as was the gospel influence in his singing and song-writing. In his autobiography Ray Charles related how his early songs were often "adaptations of spirituals" from his days at school singing in vocal quartets. In this he was not alone, there are many examples of successful black popular songs post-war which had adapted gospel favourites such as "Have Mercy Baby" by Billy Ward & the Dominoes featuring Clyde McPhatter and among Ray Charles' 'gospel' tunes were "This Little Girl of Mine", "I've Got A Women" (from the Southern Tones' "It Must be Jesus"), and "That's Why I Love Him So" by the Gospel All Stars (1953) which became "Hallelujah I Love Her So". Elsewhere in the 1960s phrases, ideas and tales from Christianity loaned themselves to songs such as Marvin Gaye's "Can I Get a Witness" (covered by the Rolling Stones), the Impressions' "People Get Ready", "Cryin' in the Chapel" by the Orioles (covered by Elvis Presley) and a big hit for the Edwin Hawkins Singers in 1968, "O Happy Day". In later years this approach has been maintained by among others, Kanye West with "Jesus Walks" with a video featuring a fictional black prison chain gang and Lauryn Hill's "To Zion".

Not everyone approved of turning the sacred into the secular. On his British tour in 1960, Josh White wrote a one-off feature about the contemporary music scene for *The Melody Maker*. On the matter of the blues he asserted that while a lot of people try to sing them "only a few know how" because it is a matter of being "a little ahead or a little after the beat". In that respect, he praised Big Bill Broonzy and Ray Charles but suggested many people did not like the way that Charles mixed "spirituals with the blues", adding it is "sacrilege" when he takes a "beloved spiritual and turns it into a sex song".

Another singer and pianist who like Duke Ellington and Ray Charles explored a broad range of black American music was Nina Simone (1933-2003) and like Ray Charles she was an influence on British bands – again notably the Animals. In April 1967 Simone appeared at Portsmouth Guildhall in a fascinating concert bill with the black American comedian and activist Dick Gregory and the English jazz/soul trio the Peddlers. The *Evening News,* described her as an "exotic coloured singer" and after the concert, 'Spinner's column suggested the audience was like a "Portsmouth Pop People's Who's Who?"

Simone's first album for RCA, *With Heart at all Times,* a collection of blues, gospel and soul tracks was released in the same month as her Portsmouth appearance and the sleeve notes (by Sid McCoy) began by focusing on her as an "individualist of the highest sort". Nina Simone, had studied at the Juilliard School of Music, New York, and comfortably crossed the boundaries of blues, jazz, folk, rhythm & blues, gospel and pop although the result was often more than the sum of those parts. She was active as an arranger and performer and also during the 'Civil Rights Sixties' was more visibly engaged in those issues than others. It would be 1968 before Simone enjoyed chart success in Britain when her version of a track from the Hippy musical *Hair,* "Ain't Got No – I Got Life" reached number two, but in the USA she had enjoyed an R&B hit record in 1958 with George Gershwin's "I Loves You Porgy" and followed this with her 1959 debut album *Little Girl Blue.* The title track was the Broadway 'classic' by Rodgers and Hart, and others from that source included an instrumental version of "You'll Never Walk Alone". There was also Ellington's "Mood Indigo" and Basie's "Good Bait", plus "My Baby Just Cares for Me", a Gus Khan song from the 1930s which would be a top ten hit for Simone in Britain in the 1980s.

One of her most popular numbers was a version of Screaming Jay Hawkins' "I'll Put A Spell on You" which was covered by organist and singer Alan Price as his first single, after leaving the Animals – he also recorded another song from Simone's repertoire "Willow Weep for Me", written in 1932 by Ann Ronell and dedicated initially to George Gershwin. Price's new group the jazz-flavoured Alan Price Set were the last act to play Portsmouth's Rendezvous Club and they also appeared at the Birdcage, but this was not Price's first encounter with Simone's music since as a member of the Animals he had enjoyed a top three hit in Britain with "Don't Let Me Be Misunderstood" a song written specifically for Simone and included on her 1964 album *Broadway-Blues-Ballads*. The music press at the time reported that Simone was not best pleased with this cover, although apparently after a verbal confrontation with Animals singer Eric Burdon, they became friends. Interestingly Simone also recorded two very different versions of the old folk song "House of the Rising Sun" which was the Animals biggest hit record (number one in June 1964). The Animals played at the Guildhall, Rendezvous and also subsequently the Savoy and perhaps performed those songs there.

Musically, Nina Simone's engagement with the Civil Rights movement probably found its most significant expression through her composition "Mississippi Goddam" a response to two appalling events in the south in 1963, the murder of Medger Evans and the September bombing of a Church in Alabama that killed four young black girls and she remained politically active, releasing a Civil Rights-influenced *In Concert* album in 1964. Bob Dylan's song "Only a Pawn in their Game" is also a direct response to the murder of Evans, while a contemporary black British singer and musician who cites Simone as a big influence is Laura Mvula who gave an accomplished, innovative performance at Southsea's Victorious Festival in 2015.

Nina Simone was a fine singer and an accomplished, inventive pianist and there is of course a long and important history of piano-playing in black American music, including other women such as Lil Hardin with Louis Armstrong, Mary Lou Williams and in more recent times Carla Bley, Alice Coltrane, Diana Krall and others. The piano has been a key instrument in all forms of black American music from ragtime, to great bandleaders like Duke Ellington and Count Basie, and the solo pianists who played in the 'juke joints', and barrelhouses between the wars. Their tunes, often instrumentals, were played with a strong left hand as eight or twelve-bar blues, which were particularly good for dancing and these pianists made many records including "Pinetop's Boogie Woogie" (Chicago 1928) by Clarence 'Pinetop' Smith, "Honky Tonk Train Blues" by Meade Lux Lewis – a British hit in 1976 for Keith Emerson – and others by Albert Ammons, Little Brother Montgomery who toured Europe and Britain more than once in the early 1960s and Pete Johnson, whose recording of "Roll 'Em Pete" with the 'blues shouter' Joe Turner (New York, 1938) is one of the seminal recordings in that style.

After the war, Joe Turner recorded sides for Atlantic Records in New York which clearly paved the way for rock & roll including "The Chicken & the Hawk", "Honey Hush"; "Flip Flop and Fly"; "TV Mama"; and "Shake, Rattle and Roll" which was covered by Bill Haley & his Comets and was their first British hit in December 1954. None of the major names in blues piano from the 1920s or 1930s visited Portsmouth but the younger Otis Spann came with Muddy Waters in 1964, while New Orleans pianist Champion Jack Dupree was an early guest of the original Birdcage Club in March 1965 and also played at the Guildhall in 1969. Dupree, an entertaining character had first recorded in Chicago in 1940 and after touring Britain and Europe he settled in this country and then in Switzerland.

Joe Turner toured Britain in the 1960s, appearing on BBC2's *Jazz 625* but he did not come to Portsmouth, although two of Count Basie's jazz and blues singers did play at the Guildhall: the very experienced Jimmy Rushing came with Buck Clayton's

All Stars in September 1959, while the younger Joe Williams, was there in October 1962 on a bill replacing a cancelled Sarah Vaughan show, with pianist George Shearing, and the Junior Mance Trio. Pianist and composer Mance played with Dizzy Gillespie (including Portsmouth in 1959), Cannonball Adderley and others, and backed Dinah Washington before forming his own trio and recording for Capitol and Atlantic Records. Joe Williams sang blues and rhythm & blues often in a big-band jazz arrangement, not least "Every Day I Have the Blues", but he was a smoother singer than his predecessors, who were often known as blues 'shouters' – Williams also drew on the Great American songbook, including, "I'm Beginning to See the Light", "A Fine Romance", "Teach Me Tonight" or "There Will Never Be Another You". The *Evening News* praised his performance and that of Junior Mance, although suggested Shearing was a "disappointment ... cold, clinical, disjointed".

F I V E

Bebop & Beyond

Miles Davis, Sarah Vaughan, Dizzy Gillespie, Joe Harriott, Roland Kirk

In March and April 1959, trumpeter Miles Davis recorded the album *Kind of Blue*, which the magazine *Jazzwise* notes "is frequently cited as the greatest jazz album of all time". With Davis on that album were saxophonists Cannonball Adderley and John Coltrane, pianists Bill Evans or Wynton Kelly, Paul Chambers on bass and drummer Jimmy Cobb. In September of the following year, just over 12 months after the album's release, the Miles Davis Quintet came to Portsmouth Guildhall with Kelly, Chambers and Cobb still present, while Sonny Stitt was the sole saxophonist replacing Coltrane and Adderley, although the latter appeared in Portsmouth with his own band in December 1960 as part of "Jazz at the Philharmonic", which also featured Dizzy Gillespie, Coleman Hawkins, Benny Carter and Don Byas.

In theory at least, the appearance of Davis was one of the Guildhall highlights in a period of just over three years when there were regular visits from some of the finest American modern jazz musicians. The only public record of Miles Davis's gig in Portsmouth comes from various pieces in the local *Evening News* and in tone and content these raise a number of questions about the reception and popularity of contemporary modern jazz in the city around sixty years ago.

The concert took place on a Sunday evening with a set that included "Bye Bye Blackbird", "On Green Dolphin Street" and "Walkin'", and reviewing the show in the next day's 'paper 'Perdido' suggested that Miles Davis, "rated by many as the greatest trumpeter in the world ...made a brief appearance at the Guildhall last night", spending "a total of about 15 minutes" on stage in each of the two sets. When asked about this, Davis apparently replied that the audience would not wish to see him standing on stage when not actually playing. Despite his reservations, 'Perdido' felt that Davis had delighted "the rather small audience with his rounded, almost sweet playing" and when he left the stage to the other members of the quintet they were "worth concentrating on" – for example Sonny Stitt offered a "vivid contrast to the meanderings of British sax men", while Paul Chambers was "outstanding' on string bass.

On the following Saturday in his regular weekly column, 'Bandbox', 'Perdido' opened with a feature on the cartoon Chipmunks' bid for the American Presidency, and followed this with a feature on Britain's answer to Duane Eddy (Jim Gunner) and ballad singer (Ed Townsend). Then he returned to Miles Davis declaring himself among those jazz fans "disappointed" with his performance. He described it as "mediocre" and Davis "far different from the brilliant modernist of his records", before perhaps more surprisingly, he criticised the rest of the quintet, suggesting Sonny Stitt "overplayed every number", Paul Chambers would have been "more at home with the Modern Jazz Quartet", and drummer Jimmy Cobb "drowned pianist Wynton Kelly with persistent loud drumming", while only Kelly "showed any outstanding talent". Having switched opinions of the quintet dramatically over a few days he then returned to the matter of Miles Davis on record, praising his latest release *Sketches of Spain* which he described as a "truly wonderful" recording by the "leading modernist", although that view he confessed had been "considerably shaken by his Guildhall showing".

Was the reaction of 'Perdido' as surprising as it now seems disappointing? In the absence of further evidence about the Portsmouth gig we can only look for responses to other nights on the tour, none of which offer anything in the way of an endorsement of his criticisms. The tour opened in Hammersmith, came on the next night to Portsmouth and then travelled to Leicester, Manchester, Liverpool, Bristol, Finsbury Park, Lewisham, Birmingham, Newcastle back to Hammersmith and finished at Kilburn, before the band departed for Paris, Stockholm and Amsterdam.

There are many live recordings of Miles Davis from around this period, including one from this tour, the Manchester (Free Trade Hall) concert, which is on You Tube. It is difficult to listen today to the total recording from that night, in excess of 90 minutes, and hear it as anything other than a fine performance, so, was it less impressive in Portsmouth? We cannot know but might it be simply that our ears (and brains) have 'caught up' over the decades with the man whose restless spirit, constantly pursued new approaches to the making of music – not always to the approval of all of his fans?

There was a review in *The Times* of the opening Hammersmith concert of that tour by writer, radio presenter and jazz musician Benny Green, whose saw things rather differently from 'Perdido'. In a long piece, headed revealingly "Giant with a Trumpet" Benny Green described how *Kind of Blue* had questioned "the tenets of jazz-making more searchingly than anything since Charlie Parker", and in so doing was "introducing into the jazz context a new aesthetic" where "every note he plays is tinged with the disturbing melancholia of a highly sophisticated and super-sensitive" musician. Green concluded, "rarely have I witnessed a more impressive concert of jazz".

This was not the only occasion when the various music columns and features in the *Evening News* criticised contemporary modern jazz. In January 1961 'Spinner' reported clumsily about "dark (*sic*) whisperings about the 'way out' experiments of Ornette Coleman, Sonny Rollins and John Coltrane" suggesting "little of value" had emerged. Two years later the 'Jazzmen' suggested, "Monk rhymes with bunk" objecting to the "cloak of mysticism" drawn around the pioneer pianist, while later that year a report about college training for jazz musicians wondered whether "jazz intellectuals are searching frantically for new approaches" thereby upsetting "natural evolution". They were also unable to understand why the MJQ "must be so serious" while by contrast, one of the most surprising local controversies occurred after the appearance by Ella Fitzgerald in the summer of 1963 with a suggestion that she merely offered "glorified pop singing", to which the response was that "too often jazz enthusiasts equate popularity with artistic compromise". More positively, by October 1963 they were arguing that jazz "has always been the music of revolution", adding the only crime of Ornette Coleman, Eric Dolphy, MJQ and British-based Joe Harriott was their "fresh approach". In their end-of-year summary of 1964 they identified four promising jazz artists Hampton Hawes, organist Jimmy Smith, Herbie Hancock and British saxophonist Tubby Hayes but they were concerned the field was "dominated by ageing jazzmen" – earlier that year they had described the Tubby Hayes Orchestra as "Britain's most progressive big band and a powerhouse of modern jazz talent".

Many of the post-war bebop musicians who revolutionised jazz had begun in the big bands of the 1930s, and while subsequently they often performed in smaller groups – not least for economic reasons – Miles Davis also worked regularly with arranger Gil Evans on studio recordings with a bigger band, and 'Dizzy' Gillespie had a big band in the late 1940s. John 'Dizzie' Gillespie arrived in Kansas City with the Cab Calloway Band in 1940, was introduced to saxophonist Charlie Parker and they continued to meet up and play, at times working together in Earl Hines' Big Band, which made a connection back to another giant of jazz, Louis Armstrong, with whom Hines had played in the 1920s – as in most musical revolutions there is a thread that takes us back to the older forms and styles. In his big band, Hines also brought in a new vocalist, Sarah Vaughan, perhaps eventually the finest bebop vocalist, especially when scatting; in January 1960 Sarah Vaughan was another who would help to launch Portsmouth's 1960s at the Guildhall, appearing with Britain's Johnny Dankworth Orchestra.

Sarah Vaughan has been described (McRae, 1987) as "the most wholly beautiful voice in all jazz history". Like so many of the finest black American singers her roots were in the local (Baptist) church after which she won an amateur contest at the famous Apollo Theatre in Harlem and when still a teenager, joined the band of pianist Earl Hines. She was an accomplished musician for whom the developments in bebop made complete sense and she brought her musical knowledge and those inno-vations to a variety of songs including her versions of other women's recordings as well as the traditional tunes of the Great American Songbook – the album entitled *My First 15 Sides* includes "It Might as well be Spring" (Rodgers & Hammerstein), "East of the Sun" (Brooks Bowman, 1934), "Mean to Me" (Fred E. Ahlert & Roy Turk 1929) another Billie Holiday song "Lover Man", Peggy Lee's "What More Can a Woman Do?", and two compositions by the leading jazz critic Leonard Feather. She also released an album *Sarah Vaughan sings Broadway: Great*

Songs from Hit Shows and in 1955 an album with the fine jazz trumpeter Clifford Brown who died in a car crash age 25 just a year after the release. The album was said to be Vaughan's favourite of her work and *Billboard* magazine praised it, suggesting "her individual phrasing, (and) her highly distinctive mannerisms are in the grooves".

In *the Evening News,* 'Spinner' described the "tremendous ovation' for Sarah Vaughan's "outstanding performance" at the Guildhall in January 1960 and she reciprocated by praising the "wonderful" Guildhall, and "your audiences". In her interview she told 'Spinner' that by contrast with America where she worked mostly in clubs with her trio, she was enjoying touring with the Johnny Dankworth Orchestra, "an exciting band". As if anticipating the comments about Ella Fitzgerald, they discussed the on-going debate between 'commercial' and jazz recordings, with some critics questioning the choice of material by singers like Vaughan but citing her performances of songs like "How High the Moon" or "Passing Strangers", she responded, "I choose the tunes I like … the critics worry".

While most jazz and big bands had typically entertained a dancing audience, smaller post-war modern jazz groups often played to listeners – especially in the small New York clubs like the Onyx or the Three Deuces. It would not be long before the young trumpeter Miles Davis participated in these performances in the Charlie Parker Quintet along with pianist Bud Powell, drummer Max Roach and others. In the immediate post-war years a number of British jazz and dance band musicians who were not attracted by the New Orleans 'revival' heard about the modern jazz being played in New York's clubs and some of them, most notably tenor saxophonist Ronnie Scott, joined the ocean liner bands to earn a living and take advantage of a night or two in New York, where they heard the new music first-hand. They were known as Geraldo's Navy, after the British band leader who organised the ocean-going bands, and they brought back what they had learned, establishing a modern jazz club in Soho in 1948 called Club Eleven, with two resident bands led by saxophonists John Dankworth and Ronnie Scott. Both men were also regular visitors to Portsmouth through the 1950s although the club closed in 1950 after a drugs raid that found a number of incriminating items.

While Scott took a boat to New York, a number of black musicians from the Caribbean were travelling east across the Atlantic, and one in particular, saxophonist Joe Harriott would become an important figure in British modern jazz performing regularly in Portsmouth through the 1950s & 1960s – including a first Guildhall appearance in December 1959 on a bill with the Modern Jazz Quartet and Ronnie Ross. In its first few years after re-opening, the Guildhall played the major role in the city in promoting the major jazz performers across a full range of traditional, mainstream and modern styles, but before that the city's club, pubs had offered live events catering for modern jazz fans.

One of the first came back in 1949, when the Rhythm Incorporated Jazz Club based in the Conservative Club, Fratton Road presented a 'bop' session featuring renowned local pianist Bill Cole and his Clubmen and later that year at the same venue 400 members and guests were entertained by saxophonists Johnny Dankworth and Don Rendell. There was also a "first" 'Bop Contest' at the Empress Ballroom, North End. In the next few years the Johnny Dankworth Seven and from 1954 the Johnny Dankworth Orchestra played various local gigs at the Empress and Savoy Ballrooms, and South Parade Pier – including the first mention in the publicity for his singer Cleo Laine. The Ronnie Scott Orchestra came to the Savoy Ballroom from 1953 onwards, while in 1955 saxophonist Tubby Hayes and his

Orchestra appeared on South Parade Pier and in 1956 at the Savoy. British vocalist Annie Ross appeared with drummer Tony Crombie's Orchestra at the Savoy and during these years the annual festival of local jazz and dance bands at the venue included at least some modern jazz from acts like the Chiz Bishop Quartet, the Trevor Nabarro Quartet, and Ron Bennett & the Club Quartet.

On 20 August 1956, the movie *Rock around the Clock* opened at the Gaumont, Southsea and three months later *the Evening News* published its first local 'Top Ten' with Johnnie Ray's "Just Walking in the Rain – a cover of a recording by the black vocal group the Prisonaires – at number one. We know now that rock & roll and 'pop' constituted a threat to the popular future of jazz but John Dankworth & Cleo Laine continued to visit the Savoy regularly, with Cleo Laine also appearing in the world premiere of the play *Flesh to a Tiger* at the Kings Theatre in 1958. In that same year, Don Rendell returned to the city to appear with his Sextet at the Savoy and also appeared at Ricky's Club which started modern sessions with local groups led by Arthur Ward, Ken Bishop and Pete Moreton.

In June 1958 the Empire Theatre, Edinburgh Road was facing demolition but not before they presented a real British modern jazz 'coup' the Jazz Couriers, featuring Tubby Hayes, and Ronnie Scott plus the Welsh stride pianist Dill Jones and his Trio. A few weeks later the Jazz Couriers were back at the Savoy and approaching Christmas, Tubby Hayes and two weeks later, Ronnie Scott, joined Portsmouth band the Ken Bishop Quintet along the coast at the Chichester Jazz Club.

Tubby Hayes died in 1973 without reaching forty and unlike his sometime collaborator Ronnie Scott whose name is still associated with his club, Hayes did not leave a legacy that is noted by most people, despite which his fine recordings are still available. But in 2019, 46 years after his death, *The Times* devoted a whole page to "This fine jazz man (who) will blow you away". The article marked the release of his 'lost' album *Grits, Beans and Greens,* and John Bungey suggested Hayes "may well be the finest jazz musician you've never heard of"; a man "who seemed to arrive with his talent fully formed". His professional career began at the age of 15 and while he was notable for his often dynamic tenor saxophone playing, he could also turn to flute or 'vibes'.

From the late 1950s, along with Fratton's Railway Hotel, and Eastney's Alma Arms a number of pubs on the outskirts of the city began presenting regular modern jazz gigs, including the Sunshine Inn in Farlington, the 'Jazz Club of Horndean' at the Ship and Bell, and the Boar's Head, Boarhunt. Among those who appeared at the Sunshine Inn, usually promoted by Jerry Allen, were Ronnie Scott, Don Rendell, Tubby Hayes, Ronnie Ross, Kathy Stobart plus American Harry Klein from the Stan Kenton Band, while tenor player Jimmy Skidmore, Kathy Stobart and Canadian tenor sax player Art Ellefson were both at the Railway Hotel, while Joe Harriott appeared in Fishbourne.

Then the Guildhall concerts started. In the first six months there were two concerts that featured popular and relatively 'cool' modern jazz groups from America, the first starring Dave Brubeck's Quartet, followed in December 1959 by the Modern Jazz Quartet. Sometimes acts like these and the Jimmy Guiffre Trio who would appear there a few months later, were linked by critics to elements of classical music, occasionally dubbing their approach 'Chamber' jazz.

Guiffre and Brubeck were white musicians and there had been a tendency, dating back almost to the first jazz recordings for mainly white band leaders to pursue links with the world of 'classical' music. The earliest significant example came with the Premiere of George Gershwin's "Rhapsody in Blue", in February 1924 at the Aeolian Hall, New York which was attended by a number of leading figures from the classical world. It was performed by Paul Whiteman's Palais Royal Orchestra and the posters described it as "an experiment in modern music". By the late 1930s a number of white leaders of the big bands, notably Benny Goodman and Artie Shaw began to present recordings and concerts which in style and content sought a kind of cooler 'respectability', also somewhat akin to the world of classical music. Goodman's band for example performed an historic concert at Carnegie Hall, New York in 1938 which was also recorded and when issued in 1950 was among the first double albums in jazz history. The concert included the band performing famous tunes in a history of jazz by composers such as Basie, Ellington Will Marion Cook, 'Fats' Waller, the Gershwin brothers, Rodgers & Hart and Irving Berlin. In 1940, Artie Shaw's Orchestra performed his composition, "Concerto for Clarinet" in the Fred Astaire film *Second Chorus*. Much live jazz was still firmly rooted in the night clubs and ballrooms and was still catering for the dancers but some of it was becoming more complex, seeking an audience willing to sit and listen rather than responding physically to the rhythms of the music.

Goodman and Shaw were mostly running big bands but in the 1940s came the bebop innovations of Dizzy Gillespie, Charlie Parker, Bud Powell, Thelonious Monk, Kenny Clarke, Miles Davis and others. Pianist John Lewis, who had studied music at university met drummer Clarke during the war and worked briefly on arrangements for a band they organised before resuming his studies in New York, where he also joined Dizzy Gillespie's Big Band. He worked on other occasions with Parker, Lester Young and then with Miles Davis as an arranger and pianist on some of the tracks he recorded in the early 1950s which came to be released under the collective title as *Birth of the Cool*. These recordings also involved the composer and arranger Gil Evans who would collaborate with Miles Davis again – for example on the 1960 album *Sketches of Spain,* which *Wikipedia* describes as "exemplary", using the briefly fashionable term "Third Stream" which brought together jazz, European classical and world music.

The vibraphone player Milt Jackson was another who had been playing with the Dizzy Gillespie Big Band and in 1951 he, Lewis, bass player Percy Heath and drummer Kenny Clarke (to be replaced by Connie Kay) recorded as the Milt Jackson Quartet before re-naming themselves the Modern Jazz Quartet (MJQ). With this underpinning of bebop, Jackson in particular, added a blues 'feel' to much of their sound, while Lewis was interested in classical (often baroque) influences. By the time MJQ came to Portsmouth in October 1961 and again September 1966, the formally-dressed quartet performed in a restrained musical style.

The tracks that were brought together as *Birth of the Cool,* were the product of informal collaborations in New York, between Miles Davis, Gil Evans, John Lewis and baritone saxophonist Gerry Mulligan. To some extent they drew on the work of band leader Claude Thornhill with whom Evans had worked through most of the 1940s, and after these musicians performed live, they recorded those seminal tracks. After the work with Miles Davis, Mulligan, strongly influenced by Thornhill, continued to perform and also became increasingly noted as an accomplished arranger and composer. In 1953 he formed a quartet with Chet Baker, which unusually had no pianist, while soon after that, he added the pianist (and trombonist) Bob Brookmeyer to his own quartet. After a period apart, Brookmeyer and Mulligan, worked again in a Concert Jazz Band and in April 1963 they appeared together at the Guildhall although the Evening News described the poorly attended evening as "disappointing", adding "the surroundings were wrong".

Miles Davis typically moved on to new challenges while 'cool' jazz became associated mainly with the MJQ plus a number of white musicians based in California, including Brubeck, Baker, Mulligan, Stan Kenton (who had come to Portsmouth in 1956), and Stan Getz, whose recording of the Bossa Nova track "Desafinado" reached number 11 in the British charts approaching Christmas 1962. Their style, more relaxed than bebop, was sometimes known as West Coast and in Britain at least perhaps the best known of them was classically-trained Dave Brubeck and his Quartet, featuring the saxophonist Paul Desmond. Brubeck's style was not one that endeared itself to every jazz critic but it did on the other hand lead to considerable commercial success in a long career and in Britain this was initially noticeable with his hit record of the instrumental "Take Five", a track on the album *Time Out* which had explored the use of various time signatures – an approach which he later suggested linked his somewhat 'refined' jazz to its roots in African work songs.

"Take Five" reached number six in the British charts in October 1961, following a number 11 slot for the album the previous summer, while another single "Unsquare Dance" was a top twenty hit in May 1962. By then he had released a follow-up album *Time Further Out* which was also a top twenty success, and on 29 November 1962 the Dave Brubeck Quartet came to Portsmouth Guildhall. A few years later Brubeck teamed up with Gerry Mulligan, but after his appearance in Portsmouth, only the return of the MJQ in 1966 brought similarly 'cool' modern jazz to the city in any major way, although locally the similarly named Modern Jazz Four included Mike Hugg, described in the *Evening News* as the best vibraphone player in the area in a group that were "playing very well indeed", especially at Gosport's Downbeat Club. Joe Harriott also received an "excellent reception" there, while in February 1962 the club attracted an audience of 800 for their "dream come true" session with Johnny Dankworth, although even that size of audience left them with a substantial financial loss. By the summer of 1963 they were able to feature Portsmouth's own Jazz Workshop 13-piece big band, led by Brian Wilson and playing the music of Kenton, Dankworth and Glenn Miller,

In terms of black music in the city, from 1963 it would be increasingly the older sounds of the blues, more recent rhythm & blues and then contemporary soul which would dominate the scene – albeit with notable interventions from some leading jazz musicians and also the efforts of local promoters. In 1964, Clarence Pier began promoting "Sunday Nights is for Modernists" with the Bill Cole Quintet and free entry; in doing so they suggested "there does not seem to be any place for modern jazz in Portsmouth at present". One man doing his best to find a home was Jerry Allen who while working in the Dockyard ran many of the modern jazz gigs. He started at the George & Dragon in Kingston Road, and Ricky's Club, before moving to the Railway Hotel until he promoted those gigs at the Sunshine Inn. This was not always an easy enterprise however. His Portsmouth Modern Jazz Club celebrated a birthday in the summer of 1960 when he reported to the *Evening News* an attendance of between 80-150 and confessed there is not "a large following for modern jazz in Portsmouth". At the time his resident quartet of local musicians comprised the hard-working Bill Cole (piano), Nelson Peters (bass), Terry Flynn (vibes) and George Good (drums) – and he was promising a guest star every Monday such as Alan Branscombe, Ronnie Ross, Bill Le Sage and others.

In 2015 Jerry Allen wrote from the home in South Africa where he relocated in 1970, with memories of Portsmouth in those days such as visits to Frank Hurlock's second hand record shop in Lake Road, when Frank was one of the local traditional jazz musicians, along with Cuff Billett, and there was also Stan Bennett, a player who ran a popular music shop near Fratton Bridge. Local musicians who worked more in the modern field included bass player Sammy Seall, Terry Flynn (vibes), pianists Mike Treend, Bob Quinton and Norman Bryant, drummers Tony Hart and Arthur Ward, and trombonist Doug Wheeler. Among the visiting British musicians, he remembered Don Rendell, Kathy Stobart, Ronnie Ross & Bert Courtley. Here is an edited but more full account of Jerry's correspondence in 2015, identifying how the world was changing in the early 1960s:

"Quite a number of our members were getting married, raising families and were no longer in weekly attendance. Not wanting the club to close I started serving in the public bar six nights a week, Saturday and Sunday lunch-times as well as to bring in a little extra cash. But alas rhythm & blues, rock & roll, and pop music was now more attractive to the youngsters and those clubs were popping up all over town. Hoping to catch at least a few of these up-and-coming youngsters we moved the club back to town at the White Hart, Kingston Crescent in the middle of town.

By now the Bill Cole group had taken up residency for the club. The next move was a short spell at the Conservative Club on the corner next to the Florist public house opposite Lake Road, where we were still having guest artists weekly. One week Bill Le Sage asked if could bring a young sax player with him, and he turned out to be the South African Dudu Pukwana. American musicians were beginning to do solo tours of English clubs so I booked Sonny Stitt with Bill Le

Sage on piano. He could not make it on a Monday our regular evening so I booked the premises for another night but the week before he was due to arrive in the country the *Melody Maker* announced that Sonny Stitt was refused a contract to play in Britain.

Soon we moved again to the Railway Hotel, where the numbers picked up enough for us to have a guest artist every Monday evening and back in town we very often had American musicians drop in if there were visiting boats tied up in the dockyard. One evening a young black sailor, a trumpeter, appeared at the door and inquired about the chances of a blow … so I let the sailor play with the interval group, which in those days was led by Mike Hugg and of course there were always some other musicians to make up a trio or quartet. After the interval the Bill Cole group would come back on and play one number before I announced the guest artist for his second set. This young sailor was bloody good so he stayed on stage after the interval. "He's not going to play with me is he?" asked Joe. The sailor was getting rapturous applause after each number and was most disappointed when I asked him to leave the stand for our guest artist's last set. The sailor came straight up to me and said sorry but he hadn't played for a while as they were at sea and his lip was just coming right. I explained to him that Joe was Britain's top alto player and our guest artist for the evening. But after Joe played the first number with Bill Cole's group the audience called for the sailor to come back on stage. Eventually, he went back on the stand. What could Joe say really? He just had to move over a bit. What an evening, although not for Joe, as this young sailor nearly blew him off the stand and I was a little surprised when Joe agreed to play for us again some time later.

At times the room at the Railway Hotel got a bit tightly packed and there was no room for anyone that wanted to dance. Ricky just over the tracks in Goldsmith Avenue approached me and said that his club was vacant on a Monday evening and there was plenty of room for those who wanted to dance as well as all the tables around the band stand for the listeners, so we moved again. On one occasion, I tried booked Kimbells and brought the Tony Kinsey group down from London. Luckily I broke even on that one, while at Ricky's I booked the Ken Simms Vintage Jazz Band to see if we could not get some trad-jazz going. Dismal failure. The "great unwashed" did not appear in any strength, while those that did appear never removed their duffle coats and made half-a-cider last all evening!

Eventually the sessions at Ricky's club petered out through lack of support. Pop music was now encroaching on all sides, but yet again I had to try, this time (1965/6) in the function room of the Cambridge Hotel in Southsea. I booked some good acts such as singer Mark Murphy, organist Alan Haven with drummer Tony Crombie, Joe Harriott and a few others and even gave trad-jazz another shot but perhaps the Cambridge Hotel behind Handley's Department Store (later Debenham's) was too 'up market'? so yet again it petered out, while across the road in Kimbells the first version of the "Birdcage" was going great guns".

In October 1966 after more attempts Jerry told the *Evening News* he was "disgusted" after just eight people showed at his latest Monday night at the Cambridge. He closed the club while elsewhere in the city other jazz clubs were struggling and the Guildhall reported low audience figures for Bud Freeman and Wingy Manone. Jerry concluded his thoughts suggesting "but then that was pop music", although blues, rhythm & blues and later soul/Motown were not 'mainstream' pop and the man at the heart of the Birdcage Club (1965-1967), Rikki Farr, while not prioritising jazz, was responsible for some very interesting initiatives later in the decade, including jazz nights at the Brave New World which in the same Eastney premises succeeded the Birdcage over around 12 months from the end of 1967 where there was a brief, not successful experiment with some British jazz acts.

By the late 1960s, after more than twenty years of bebop and 'hard' bop, few of the most accomplished British jazz musicians were at the cutting edge of jazz, especially the black American jazz of the new generation, sometimes called 'Free Jazz' and in some cases linked closely to the decade's Civil Rights move-ment. These musicians followed John Coltrane and included Ornette Coleman, Albert Ayler, Cecil Taylor, Eric Dolphy, and Archie Shepp, none of whom appeared in Portsmouth, but there were two very interesting events in 1969, both promoted by Rikki Farr at the King's Theatre. In each case he matched one of the new more progressive rock acts with innovative jazz musicians – the first was American Rahsaan Roland Kirk with the Soft Machine, and the second featuring Alexis Korner, plus Joe Harriott, John Mayer and Indo-Jazz Fusions, a band that brought together Harriott's Quintet with Mayer's five classically-trained Indian musicians.

The evening with multi-instrumentalist Roland Kirk (1935-1977) was particularly interesting. To a large extent it attracted a young audience who had grown through the 1960s listening mostly to the songs of guitar-based pop and rhythm & blues or American soul and Motown, yet here was a man who played instrumentals, demonstrating an extraordinary mastery of circular breathing and sometimes playing three instruments simultaneously. His main 'conventional' jazz instruments were tenor saxophone and flute to which he added stritch, manzello, nose flute and sometimes piano or percussion and he drew on a broad range of musical influences including ragtime, blues and older jazz styles but also classical music. In recordings he made in the 1970s he often used electronic and found sounds in a manner similar to experiments in the world of (mostly white) avant garde American and European music. On stage he would often launch into polemical political statements not least about the Civil Rights movement of that period.

By the time of these King's Theatre concerts, Rikki Farr's hugely influential presence in the city in the second half of the 1960s was nearly at an end, although he played a major role in the three big Isle of Wight Festivals just across the Solent and while August 1970 is strictly speaking just outside the focus of this decade it brings us back to our opening of this chapter, and the appearance at the last, huge event of Miles Davis with a band that included keyboard players Chick Corea and Keith Jarrett, drummer Jack de Johnette and Britain's Dave Holland who, in early experiments with a form of jazz funk put away his string bass in favour of an electric bass guitar. After Miles Davis and his band had played, he was asked by the film crew for the name of the one piece they performed, to which he replied "Call It Anything" – so they did.

S I X

Everyday I Have the Blues

BB King, John Lee Hooker, Jimmy Reed, Little Walter, British R & B.

1963 opened with one of the fiercest winters in living memory – it had begun on Boxing Day and ran through to early March, as snow and ice disrupted normal life and decimated sporting events. The British pop world meanwhile, was dominated by a home-grown act, Cliff Richard & the Shadows, and from the USA Elvis Presley, and the pair were surrounded for the most part by solo singers and guitar-led instrumental groups. The 'Twist' was a fading force on the dance floor and so too 'Trad' as a Hit Parade phenomenon, with Kenny Ball's Jazzmen enjoying just about the genre's last top ten hit at the start of the year with a Japanese song, "Sukiyaki".

Cliff and Elvis survived but others gave way to the sounds of Liverpool's Merseybeat notably the Beatles of course but also Gerry & the Pacemakers, the Searchers, the Swinging Blue Jeans, the Merseybeats and Billy J Kramer & the Dakotas – plus Cilla Black. Simultaneously and further south there was another musical revolution, not yet in the pop charts but initially in the London area's jazz clubs as a new generation of fans, with mods at their core, flocked to see and hear the latest British R&B groups. Like those from Liverpool they were mostly young, white, and with a sound that initially prioritised electric guitars and harmonicas rather than the pianos and brass, reed and wind instruments that had been at the core of so much previous black American music heard in Britain. They were also more resistant to the 'showbiz' look of stage uniforms which was still common among the northern groups.

While the R&B groups were mostly young, there were two 'father figures', guitarist Alexis Korner, and harmonica player Cyril Davies who had switched from 'Leadbelly-style' 12-string guitar. They led this new British blues sound, which differed from the previous home-grown, jazz-based blues singing of Ottilie Patterson (with Chris Barber), George Melly (with Mick Mulligan) Beryl Bryden and Ken Colyer. Korner and Davies, like Colyer, had been important participants in the skiffle scene of the mid-1950s but also like Colyer, they moved on as it became a commercial and somewhat less 'authentic' teenage craze. Korner and Davies then formed the Blues Incorporated, recording the first British 'blues' album in 1962 with the some-what misleading title *R&B from the Marquee* since it was a studio recording, and they also gave opportunities to young musicians to perform with them on live gigs – among them, members of the Rolling Stones, plus Paul Jones (Manfred Mann) and Long John Baldry, one of the featured vocal-ists on the album that included songs by Leroy Carr, Jimmy Witherspoon and the prolific Chess records bass player and songwriter Willie Dixon.

As Blues Incorporated with saxophonist Dick Heckstall-Smith developed a more jazz-oriented sound, Cyril Davies left in 1963 and recruited his own group, the All-Stars. They made various recordings including his seminal harmonica instrumental "Countryline Special" on an EP which also included the vocal track "Chicago Calling" which might serve as the theme tune for these new R&B groups – led most obviously by the Rolling Stones but also including the Yardbirds, the Pretty Things,

Downliners Sect and others. Sadly, in January 1964, just short of his 32nd birthday, and as his 'Chicago-style' British R&B began to make headway in Britain, Cyril Davies died. As a consequence, he never played in Portsmouth, although he and the All-Stars appeared regularly on the ABC television folk series *Hullabaloo*, sometimes with Long John Baldry on vocals. After his untimely death the band reformed as Long John Baldry & the Hoochie Coochie Men (usually with Rod Stewart on second vocals) and they appeared regularly at the Rendezvous Club in 1964 – including an interesting collaboration between that club and Gosport's Downbeat when they appeared together with Georgie Fame & the Blues Flames at Thorngate Hall. In 1965 Long John Baldry reunited with Rod Stewart and together with singer Julie Driscoll and organist Brian Auger and the Trinity created the revue-style Steam Packet – more soul-oriented than the earlier blues bands. Steam Packet visited Portsmouth on a number of occasions, playing the Guildhall, Savoy and Birdcage and a couple of years later Baldry brought his new band Bluesology to South Parade Pier including pianist Reg Dwight (Elton John).

London's developing R&B club scene was based in venues like the Marquee, Crawdaddy, Eel Pie Island, 100 Club or Studio 51, and while there was a distinct difference in material between the bands playing there and the chart-topping Merseybeat and northern groups, the one common source was probably Chuck Berry since most of these groups covered his songs in their early days. But while the Beatles and their contemporaries often covered early rock & roll or recent vocal group recordings, including a number by 'girl' groups, the London R&B groups drew more heavily on solo vocal performances by black urban blues singers, particularly those from Chicago's Chess label such as Muddy Waters, Howlin' Wolf, Sonny Boy Williamson, and Bo Diddley.

The Rolling Stones had taken their name from a Muddy Waters recording, his version of an older "Catfish Blues", while the 'B' side of their first single (Chuck Berry's "Come On") was another Muddy Waters track "I Want to be Loved", and on their first two albums they covered his recordings of "I Just Want to Make Love to You" and "I Can't be Satisfied". On radio broadcasts they also played Buster Brown's "Fannie Mae", Tommy Tucker's "Hi Heel Sneakers", Bo Diddley's "Cops & Robbers", Howlin' Wolf's "Down in the Bottom" and a number of other Chuck Berry songs including "Beautiful Delilah", "Roll Over Beethoven" and "Memphis Tennessee". Chuck Berry would not appear in Portsmouth until 1991, but all these R&B groups played in the city in the mid-1960s, with the Rolling Stones coming first to the Savoy Ballroom in September 1963, one night after Manfred Mann at Kimbells, and then twice to the Guildhall. In February 1964 they were supporting on a package tour starring pop singers Mike Sarne and John Leyton, plus Liverpool acts the Merseybeats and Swinging Blue Jeans, but by July of the following year they were the headline act with the Walker Brothers, Elkie Brooks and Steam Packet.

Muddy Waters' early visits to Britain were complicated by the question of whether audiences did or did not wish to hear him playing electric guitar – with less of an impact it somewhat anticipated the controversy looming over Bob Dylan's transformation. When the *Evening News* published its evaluation of popular music at the end of 1962 they anticipated "the return of music", suggesting the dominance of guitars "will soon be over" replaced among other styles by "sophisticated Bossa Nova". They concluded "confidently" that soon "we shall see the end of the guitar". They were not quite right.

In the blues field one of the reasons electric guitars held firm was the emergence in the 1960s of a number of younger black

Americans who would influence the sound of British blues as the decade progressed, among them Buddy Guy, Magic Sam, Otis Rush and the so-called (unrelated) 'Three Kings', Freddy, Albert and eventually most famous of all, Riley, better known as BB King who, like Albert, would appear at Portsmouth Guildhall in 1969. During the mid/late 1960s, the leading British blues band John Mayall's Bluesbreakers with their succession of influential guitarists Eric Clapton, Peter Green and Mick Taylor, covered recordings by a number of those men including "All Your Love" (Otis Rush), "Born Under a Bad Sign" (Albert King) and three Freddy King instrumentals "Hideaway" (Clapton), "The Stumble" (Green) and "Driving Sideways" (Taylor).

BB King who would become the biggest name among these electric guitarists was rarely covered by British bands but the 'King' style with the bent single notes became almost commonplace among British guitarists of a certain generation. It is probable that BB King had a limited impact on the British R&B musicians in the 1960s because he was simply less visible. Some of his recordings were released on the British Sue label by Guy Stevens but American academic Charles Keil in his 1966 book *Urban Blues* noted that he had at that point never toured Europe and even in the USA, had "never done a college concert or appeared at a folk club … never been on a jazz festival stage" and hardly ever "directed his efforts towards a pop or teenage market".

BB King was born in Itta Bena Mississippi, the son of sharecroppers; he worked in the cotton fields and sang and later played guitar in local gospel church choirs. Pursuing a career in music he moved to Memphis and began playing in small venues or working as a DJ on local radio. He was related to and cared for in those early days by the older Mississippi blues singer/guitarist

'Bukka' White who came to Britain in 1967. BB King began featuring on local radio and was nicknamed the Beale Street Blues Boy, which was eventually shortened to BB. Some of his earliest recordings were produced by Sam Phillips, the man who first recorded Elvis Presley, and BB King assembled a bigger band than most blues singers, including three saxophones, as he became one of the hardest working touring and recording musicians from the 1950s with an R&B Chart number one in 1952 with "3 O'clock Blues". Many hits followed – indeed in 1970 he received a Grammy for his song "The Thrill is Gone" – a year after he had toured the U.S.A. as support for the Rolling Stones along with the Ike & Tina Turner Revue. Fortunately BB King had departed before the final date, the infamous Altamont free concert.

One of the older style guitar players who was an influence on the British R&B scene in the 1960s was John Lee Hooker (1917- 2001). Like Muddy Waters, he was born in Clarksdale Mississippi, was just one year younger and albeit with a distinct, less assertive sound sometimes offered a stylistic 'bridge' between the older, acoustic pre-war blues guitarists and the more recent ensemble-based, urban players. Hooker started recording in Detroit in 1948 and his records were released on various labels through his career including Crown, Vee-Jay, Modern and Chess. Hooker visited Britain regularly and appeared at one of Kimbell's new R&B nights in June 1964, the first year of regular blues and R&B gigs in the city – later in the 1960s he returned to the Guildhall and South Parade Pier. Around 1963/4, two particular John Lee Hooker tracks were covered by British groups, "Dimples" (the Spencer Davis Group's first single) and "Boom Boom" (the Animals) although his somewhat idiosyncratic style, often playing one chord boogies and frequently ignoring the strict structures of 12-bar blues, sometimes made imitation and accompaniment difficult for British musicians. The boogie style would be extended most successfully a few years later by the American band Canned Heat – in 1970 they recorded together in Los Angeles.

Jimmy Reed (1925-1976) who first recorded in Chicago in 1953 was also influential in those early days and he played at Kimbells in 1964. In America, Jimmy Reed usually recorded with a small group, often including guitarist Eddie Taylor mainly for the Vee-Jay label, sometimes for Bluesway. He played guitar and harmonica together, the latter in a harness, and was influential not least because he generally played straightforward twelve-bar blues with little fancy instrumentation, often with a loping rhythm. Among the groups that covered his songs, the Rolling Stones included "Honest I Do" on their first LP, and played a live version of "Ain't that Loving You Baby" on the BBC. Other covers included Downliners Sect whose first single was "Baby What's Wrong", the Pretty Things with "Big Boss Man" as the 'B' side of their first hit "Rosalyn", Van Morrison and Them recorded "Baby What You Want Me to Do" and "Bright Lights Big City" which was also on the Animals' second album, while the sound and structure of Reed's song "Shame, Shame, Shame" was copied by the Rolling Stones for their 'B' side "Little by Little". In 1969, they performed Reed's "Sun is Shining" at the Altamont free concert – it proved to be somewhat wishful thinking. In November 1964 Jimmy Reed appeared at Kimbells, backed by John Lee's Groundhogs, one of the regular backing bands for visiting American blues singers, although locally there was little publicity for the gig and subsequently no mention in *the Evening News* who seemed more interested in an appearance that week at the Rendezvous by one of the bands most indebted to him, Downliners Sect. During the tour he was interviewed by John Holt for Mick Vernon's British 'fanzine' *R&B Monthly,* telling Holt his sound was "down-home cotton patch blues" while

Holt added the view that Reed's "wide appeal" was a result of his "unique combination of City and Country blues" – part Mississippi and part Chicago.

Despite his considerable influence on the British sound of that time (1963/4) he was rarely accorded the same critical admiration of many of his contemporaries and too often his material was ignored. In a *Jazz Monthly* review (August 1967) of a new release titled *The New Jimmy Reed Album* the leading British blues researcher Paul Oliver suggested "if anyone is an uncompromised Urban singer it is Reed" although noting he was not one of the older blues singer to be adopted by the largely acoustic folk festival scene in the USA. Oliver conceded that while some of his records had been "disappointing" he "always sounds authentically himself" and a year after Oliver's review, Jimmy Reed was in London on the "American Folk-Blues Festival '68" along with John Lee Hooker, T-Bone Walker and others, one eight nights of *Jazz Expo 68,* subtitled "The Newport Jazz Festival in London". One of the other nights, intriguingly titled "The Story of Soul", featured Joe Simon, the Horace Silver Quintet, the Muddy Waters Blues Band with Otis Spann and the Stars of Faith.

In September 1964, the year that Muddy Waters' played at the Guildhall, a former member of his outstanding Chicago band, harmonica player Little Walter came to Portsmouth's Rendezvous Club. Photos of the tour on another night, in Cambridge, show him playing guitar or harmonica – he is the only harmonica player to be inducted into the Rock & Roll Hall of Fame – suggesting that on that tour he played familiar instrumentals ("Juke", "Thunderbird", "Off the Wall") plus songs like "My Babe", "Last Night" and "Blues with a Feeling". At the Rendezvous he too was backed by John Lee's Groundhogs.

The sudden, unexpected popularity of the British R&B groups, some in the clubs, but others led by the Rolling Stones in the pop charts, introduced recent or contemporary, mostly vocal black American music to a new teenage audience, not least perhaps when the Rolling Stones took their cover of the Willie Dixon song "Little Red Rooster" to the top of the charts in late 1964 – the only British number one for a blues song, which was previously recorded by Howlin' Wolf and Sam Cooke. While the members of many of these new London-based R&B groups like the Rolling Stones were from the south-eastern corner of England there were also a number of successful northern and midlands-based R&B groups who re-located to London and became part of that club scene. These included the Animals (from Newcastle), John Mayall (Manchester) and the Spencer Davis Group and the Moody Blues from Birmingham, all of whom featured keyboards to greater or lesser extent. There was another strand of live club acts by 1964 more jazz-oriented, featuring (usually Hammond) organs plus a brass/reed section. They included Georgie Fame & the Blue Flames, Zoot Money's Big Roll Band, Long John Baldry & the Hoochie Coochie Men and the Graham Bond Organisation; Georgie Fame and Zoot Money were particularly popular in Soho's Flamingo Club where a black audience, mixed with young mods. Alto saxophonist Bond had switched to keyboards – including the new Mellotron – and vocals, having recently played modern jazz with regular Portsmouth visitor Don Rendell and for a brief period his band included jazz guitarist John McLaughlin although mostly they used Jack Bruce on a six-string bass guitar, adding Dick Heckstall-Smith on saxophones.

Among the new British groups there was one with strong local links, named after their keyboard player, the South African Manfred Mann. Their origins were as an instrumental modern jazz group including drummer Mike Hugg but after adding a Portsmouth-born singer, Paul Pond, who adopted the stage name Paul Jones, they were initially the Blues Brothers. In 1963, as another of the new R&B groups playing on the national club scene, they appeared in a residency at the Railway Hotel every Thursday where they were reviewed by the 'Jazzmen' in the *Evening* News in July. They were not particularly free with compliments, despite predicting "big things", describing the band playing "the loudest and most blatantly commercial" R&B with only the "vaguest relations with jazz". They were critical of the "fairly moronic and unimaginative" organist Manfred Mann although felt the harmonica playing of Paul Jones offered "brief intervals" of the blues but confessed having no way "to judge material such as Chuck Berry's "Sweet Little Sixteen"". A few weeks later in his *Evening News* pop column, 'Spinner' defended the group, and predicted success in the pop market, describing their first single "Why Should We Not?" under their new name Manfred Mann as "exciting and original".

The band continued to appear at various local venues most weeks, often promoted by Southampton's Concorde Club, and including the Railway Hotel, Fratton and Kimbells Ballroom, Osborne Road, Southsea where on special nights, "Ladies" were admitted for 2/6d (12.5p) before 8.30 pm. The band's first album *The Five Faces of Manfred Mann* would not be released until the autumn of 1964 but it was indicative of their stage material in those R&B club days with covers of familiar R&B tracks like "Smokestack Lightning" (Howlin' Wolf), "Hoochie Coochie Man" and "Got My Mojo Working" by Muddy Waters and "Bring It to Jerome" (Bo Diddley) as well as showing their jazz origins with Cannonball Adderley's "Sack of Woe", a 1940s rhythm & blues track "Down the Road Apiece" (Amos Milburn) and the Ike & Tina Turner hit "It's Gonna Work out Fine". The latter hinted at a shift towards covers of other more melodic soul tracks, which would soon include their chart hits "Come Tomorrow" (Marie Knight) and "Oh No Not My Baby" (Maxine Brown).

The London club scene gave regular opportunities to the new R&B acts in 1963, although bookings in the provinces and record releases would increase in the following year. In the summer of 1963, the Rolling Stones released their first single while recordings by the original American blues singers also appeared more frequently mostly on LPs, including a number of interesting budget-priced compilations. There also a brief period during 1964 when a number of them saw single releases edging into the lower reaches of the British charts and most, while touring, also appeared on British television. The 45 rpm successes began in the spring of 1964 with a little known pianist and singer Tommy Tucker whose record, "Hi Heel Sneakers", was covered by many British R&B groups, and reached the top thirty. In November 1964 he appeared at Portsmouth Guildhall on a tour that mixed British R&B group the Animals, 1950s Sun-label rocker Carl Perkins plus Elkie Brooks and the Nashville Teens. John Lee Hooker matched Tucker's spot at 23 with "Dimples" in June and there were a couple that made it into the top fifty, Howlin' Wolf's "Smokestack Lightnin'" (June) and Jimmy Reed's "Shame, Shame, Shame" (September), while Sonny Boy Williamson's album *Down and Out Blues* reached number 20 in the album charts in mid-summer.

With their growing popularity, these blues singers toured and appeared on a variety of television shows. During 1964, John Lee Hooker appeared on BBC's *Beat Room, Ready Steady Go!* (twice), and even *Top of the Pops* singing "Dimples", when Louis Armstrong was on the same show with "Hello Dolly". Howlin' Wolf and his guitarist Hubert Sumlin appeared on *The Beat Room,* as did Tommy Tucker, Memphis Slim, and Little Walter on two occasions; Little Walter also appeared on *Ready Steady Go!* so too, Jimmy Witherspoon and Chuck Berry. There were also television series and specials during the year, not least the *Blues & Gospel Train* and a live concert by Ray Charles on ITV in August. In the same month BBC2's *Jazz 625* broadcast live from the Richmond Jazz & Blues Festival.

There had been jazz festivals before in Britain, such as those at Beaulieu where one or two blues musicians appeared including Memphis Slim and James Cotton, one of the successors to Little Walter as the harmonica player for Muddy Waters. The 1964 broadcast was the fourth annual festival at Richmond which in the early years featured almost exclusively the British jazz acts that were seen in Portsmouth, such as Chris Barber, Don Rendell, John Dankworth, Joe Harriott, Ronnie Ross, Tubby Hayes, Ken Colyer, Kenny Ball, Humphrey Lyttleton and others. Ottilie Patterson had appeared with Chris Barber but the first recognition of the new British R&B scene came in the 1963 festival with appearances by Cyril Davies & the All-Stars, Long John Baldry and the Rolling Stones. By August 1964 the shift from jazz towards R&B indicated this new audience, with a bill including Mose Allison, Memphis Slim and Jimmy Witherspoon from the USA, plus the Rolling Stones, Georgie Fame & the Blue Flames, Long John Baldry & the Hoochie Coochie Men, the Graham Bond Organisation, Manfred Mann, the T-Bones and the Yardbirds (with Eric Clapton). By 1965, the handout for the festival noted, "Something unheard of is happening at Richmond ... for the first time ... the pure jazz-men are outnumbered by beat and rhythm-and-blues groups who are no strangers to the hit parade".

This shift was clearly demonstrated at two Portsmouth venues during 1964. In 1963 the original Rendezvous jazz club had closed for a few months before an announcement in the

Evening News at Christmas that it would be re-opening on Saturday nights in February 1964 in the Oddfellows Hall, Kingston Road with a new focus on R&B – a focus it would share with Sunday and midweek gigs at Kimbells Ballroom, Southsea, some organised by Southampton's Concorde Club. The Kimbell's R&B Sunday nights opened in January 1964 with a brief residency from Georgie Fame, while according to the *Evening News* the Rendezvous "roared in" with Jimmy Powell & the Five Dimensions and then Alexis Korner's Blues Incorporated. They followed that with the Graham Bond Organisation playing "dynamic R&B with a definite leaning towards modern jazz", Downliners Sect, the Animals, the Pretty Things, the Hoochie Coochie Men, Georgie Fame & the Blue Flames, the Soul Agents, the Spencer Davis Group and the T-Bones. In *the Evening News*, the 'Jazzmen's' weekly column noted John Mayall's "excellent reception" and praised the "fairly authentic" material and "refusal to pander to the commercial element in rhythm & blues". In May 1965 when Eric Clapton, appeared at the Rendezvous, with Mayall's band it was reported as "a triumph".

Kimbells presented some of the same acts as the Rendezvous, plus Zoot Money's Big Roll Band, Alex Harvey, Chris Farlowe, the Yardbirds, the Art Woods and former Blues Incorporated vocalist Ronnie Jones, with his band the Nightimers. Jones was a black United States airman, who was stationed and then settled in Britain and by the mid-sixties other British-based soul bands with black singers who now lived in Britain included Geno Washington (and the Ram Jam Band) and Herbie Goins (and the Night-timers) from the USA, and Jimmy James & the Vagabonds and Errol Dixon (& the Honeydrippers) from Jamaica. They all played in Portsmouth with Jones, Goins, Washington and James regulars particularly at the Birdcage.

As these two venues gathered more followers in the early months of 1964, *the Evening News* reported a new controversy, asking whether this predominantly British R&B was "genuine". Some considered it "authentic music with blues roots" while others thought it "watered down". Since to that point many live performances by American blues musicians had been to seated concert audiences they were also other questions about dancing, while some enjoyed themselves and could not understand why that was a problem. The long-term Rendezvous promoter Ernie Sears retorted that he was not seeking to "satisfy the purists ... we cater for a larger number" but the 'purists' were insisting that groups led by Alexis Korner and Graham Bond had "little connection with rhythm & blues". Local musician, fan and record shop proprietor Frank Hurlock told *the Evening News* that British R&B was "nothing less than a shook-up potion of rock & roll" adding that "the bookers and agents know it". Hurlock believed they were the same people who had recently "flaunted traditional jazz" and accused them of caring about the money, not the music.

The Sunday nights at Kimbells gave opportunities to local R&B groups, in particular the J Crow Combo and the Shamrocks (IOW), a practice adopted by the Rendezvous in October 1964 when the Sons of Man (future Aubrey Small) first appeared as a support act. Two months later after a support to the (original) Moody Blues, 'Spinner' noted that the headliners featured an "unusual" electric piano ("what next, electric drums?") while the Sons of Man swapped instruments on some numbers to allow their bass guitarist to play flute. They were one of the regular groups in that support role at the club, along with the Roadrunners who would become Simon Dupree & the Big Sound, the Challengers and from 1965 the Soul Society.

The choice of the Soul Society even in a support role was indicative of another shift in the kind of black American music that was becoming popular in Britain in the mid-1960s. The black American musicians who appeared in Portsmouth in 1964 were all from the blues field but in America black music had been undergoing a transition during and following the mid-1950s explosion of rock & roll. At Chess Records for example the success of men like Muddy Waters and Howlin' Wolf had waned somewhat as Chess put more energies into the new generation of doo-wop vocal groups and soul singers – plus Bo Diddley and Chuck Berry, the latter with his incomparable anthems to teenage dreams. In Detroit, Berry Gordy pursued a similar policy with the development of Tamla Motown which was never a blues label and sought a 'crossover' audience. The revival of interest in the older blues singers among a young white British audience was sustained but only in 1964 was it a 'pop' phenomenon, although there would be a second 'blues boom' in the late 1960s and some performers like Muddy Waters and John Lee Hooker maintained a successful career for some time beyond the 1960s – not least collaborating with white rock musicians for whom they were once heroes and musical role models.

S E V E N

Dancing in the Street

The Platters, Drifters, Beatles, Motown

A great deal of jazz is instrumental music, while most of the great jazz singers perform solo or perhaps in duets; the blues too, predominantly vocal, mostly features solo singers. There is however a major tradition of black American ensemble singing, sometimes with a featured soloist, in gospel, the work-song and other popular styles. While these styles developed mostly in the USA, David Olusoga's comprehensive history of black Britain records how black American musicians were visiting Britain in Victorian times, including "the most important of the black American musical troupes" the "legendary" Fisk Jubilee Singers who came from Tennessee first in 1873 and introduced local audiences "to the world of Negro spirituals". They returned in 1875 and 1884 and performed to Queen Victoria. In the popular idiom, the Unique Quartette's "Mama's Black Baby Boy" from the autumn of 1893 is one of the earliest, if not the first black record-ings (on a cylinder) to have been issued and their *a cappella* ensemble harmony style is part of that tradition leading in the 1930s & 1940s to popular black American vocal groups including the Mills Brothers, the Ink Spots, the Ravens, the Delta Rhythm Boys and the Golden Gate Quartet. From their approach – whether sanctified or secular – came the black vocal groups that had such a huge impact on popular music through the 1950s and 1960s.

One of the earliest black vocal groups to make a mark on Britain's new record charts, the Platters, were four men and a woman who enjoyed hit records in the USA in 1956, with "Only You" and "The Great Pretender" – not only in the R&B charts but also in the pop hit parade. Initially the Platters did not have a British record company and found those hits covered here respectively by the Hilltoppers (reaching number three) and Jimmy Parkinson (number nine), but before the end of the year the songs were released in Britain as a double-sided hit on Mercury, reaching number five and shortly after that the group's album track "My Prayer" was released and reached the British top five. They had two more top three hits in 1958 with "Twilight Time" and a year later when "Smoke Gets in Your Eyes" reached number one. In January 1960, the Platters reached the British Top Twenty for the last time with "Harbor Lights", a version featuring the recorded sounds of ship bells ringing, and ocean waters splashing. Intriguingly the lyrics had been written by Irishman Jimmy Kennedy after he had stopped in the Harbour Lights pub at the top of Portsmouth Harbour on his way to meet his mother from a ship in Southampton.

In the same month the Platters became the first of these new vocal groups to visit Portsmouth, opening the decade at the Guildhall on 19 January 1960. *The Evening News* under the headline "Platters Achieve Guildhall Triumph", reported "two packed houses", and a "varied programme of well-chosen standard 'pop' tunes and comedy numbers". The group offered "showmanship and personality" and despite a "generally quiet" audience, received "prolonged applause" in conclusion for a set that included "Twilight Time", "Smoke Gets in Your Eyes" and "The Saints".

The Platters were not the only black American vocal group to enjoy chart success in Britain in the early 1960s. The Drifters, who would appear at Portsmouth's Birdcage Club in January 1966 had enjoyed R&B chart success in 1950s USA, and entered the top thirty with their first British hit, "Dance with Me", followed at Christmas 1960 with "Save the Last Dance for Me" which reached number two in the charts. While there were no more big hits for them through that decade, other British acts covered their songs including the Searchers with their first big hit "Sweets for My Sweet", Jimmy Justice who reached the top ten with "When My Little Girl is Smiling" and the Rolling Stones who covered "Under the Boardwalk" on their second album. In their early days the Drifters had two notable lead singers who would pursue solo careers, Clyde McPhatter and Ben E King and after they departed there was often more than one group called the Drifters playing somewhere in the world, including Portsmouth's Birdcage Club – and most were highly competent at delivering their hits and well-known songs.

In the spring of 1961, the Marcels reached number one in Britain with their doo-wop version of "Blue Moon" and they attempted to kill two birds with "Merry Twist-Mas" the following December. "Blue Moon" followed the Shirelles' "Will You Still Love Me Tomorrow" which reached number four and the flip side of that single "Boys" was performed by Ringo Starr in the Beatles' live concerts and on their first album, which also featured the Shirelles' "Baby It's You". Between 1962-1964 another 'girl group' the Chiffons enjoyed hit records as did two Phil Spector-produced acts, the Crystals, who came to the Guildhall and the Ronettes.

For a brief spell the most popular of those black American vocal groups in Britain was probably the Coasters. They reached the top thirty in September 1957 with "Searchin'", six years later a hit for the Hollies who played both the Guildhall and the Birdcage. Later the Coasters hit with humour and mystery in

"Yakety Yak", "Charlie Brown" (number six in 1959) and "Poison Ivy" – the latter covered by the Rolling Stones, Manfred Mann and Dave Clark Five all of whom appeared at the Guildhall, which during 1963 & 1964 offered a variety of styles and genres in the broad field of popular music. In addition to the Crystals, among the black American artists appearing there were Little Eva, Dionne Warwick, the Isley Brothers, and Tommy Tucker, plus Millie (Small) from Jamaica. Among the newer British acts who had graduated from clubs to concert tours, the Beatles returned towards Christmas 1963 (having also played at the Savoy back in April), followed by the Animals, and Manfred Mann who shared the bill with Bill Haley in October 1964. The *Evening News* suggested Manfred Mann's version of Howlin' Wolf's "Smokestack Lightnin'" was the "most memorable number" of the night but sadly considered Bill Haley now part of "history …the magic has gone".

There was an interesting, if little-noticed evening at the Savoy in October 1964 with an appearance by Liverpool vocal group The Chants. They drew on the influence of American acts like doo-wop group the Del Vikings, plus Johnny Otis, Little Richard and The Miracles. They were the only black Merseybeat group of those times and while they never enjoyed the success of their white contemporaries they were the foundation of the Real Thing who did enjoy hit records in the 1970s including "You to Me are Everything".

In December 1964 'Spinner's' *Evening News* column surveyed the pop year just gone, noting the "influence" of *Ready Steady Go!*, describing the Rolling Stones as "earthy (and) brutal" and suggesting Tamla Motown acts were now "favourites with the way-out with its". By 1965 these newer soul and Tamla Motown acts had begun to enjoy commercial success in Britain thanks not least to appearances on British television. Among those featured in programmes like *Beat Room, Ready Steady Go!* and *Granada's Scene at 6.30* in late 1964 were Marvin Gaye, the Isley Brothers, the Miracles, Rufus Thomas and Lou Johnson ("Always Something there to Remind Me"), while the black women singers and vocal groups included Mary Wells, the Ronettes, Martha & the Vandellas and Dionne Warwick, who also appeared on ITV's *Thank Your Lucky Stars. Ready Steady Go!* featured the Dixie Cups, Sugar Pie De Santo, Kim Weston, the Soul Sisters and the Vandellas, while the Supremes appeared more than once on *Top of the Pops,* as did Fontella Bass with her Chess soul 'classic' "Rescue Me".

Like the older blues singers, to some extent these newer soul and Motown acts had popular British groups to thank for this breakthrough – not least the Beatles, who first appeared in Portsmouth on 30 March 1963, closing the first half of a package tour starring two recent American hitmakers, Chris Montez ("Let's Dance") and Tommy Roe ("Sheila" and "The Folk Singer"). By the time the tour arrived in Portsmouth, the American duo were battling to justify their status with the Beatles currently enjoying their first big hit record "Please, Please Me". At Portsmouth they played just six songs but their live and radio sets and tracks on their first album and EPs included a number of covers of black American acts including "Money" (Barrett Strong), "Twist & Shout" (Isley Brothers), "Too Much Monkey Business" and "Roll Over Beethoven" (Chuck Berry), "Hippy Hippy Shake" (Chan Romero), "Anna" (Arthur Alexander), "Chains" (the Cookies), "Boys" and "Baby It's You" (the Shirelles), "Long Tall Sally" (Little Richard), "Slow Down" (Larry Williams), "Devil in his Heart" (the Donays), "You've Really Got a Hold on Me" (the Miracles) and "Please Mr Postman" (the Marvelettes).

1964 was a rich year for black American singers visiting the Guildhall, including Muddy Waters, Ella Fitzgerald, Ray

Charles, and Sister Rosetta Tharpe, while the clubs had visits from John Lee Hooker, Jimmy Reed and Little Walter. By 1965 there was a shift away from the older blues and jazz singers towards younger black performers whose often sophisticated performances were making a mark on the pop charts. This change was anticipated in November 1964 with the visit of Dionne Warwick who made a number of fine versions of the songs of Burt Bacharach and Hal David, including "I Say a Little Prayer", "Walk on By", "Do You Know the Way to San Jose", "Don't Make Me Over" and "Anyone Who Had a Heart". Warwick appeared on a mixed bill with Merseybeat's Searchers, British group the Zombies and the Isley Brothers who had first attracted attention in Britain through covers of their songs "Twist and Shout" (the Beatles) and "Shout" (Lulu & the Luvvers). The Isley Brothers were another vocal group with its roots in gospel and having moved from their home in Ohio to New York they recorded for various labels including a short spell in the mid-1960s with Tamla Motown where at least two of their recordings "This Old Heart of Mine" and "I Guess I'll Always Love You" were destined to become dancers' favourites and classic tracks from the Detroit label. They were also typical of the kinds of records that would be playing in the clubs as 1965 arrived and contemporary soul began to replace the older blues acts as the favoured sounds of the mods and the dancers.

As with most stylistic fashions, the change was not instant. 1965 opened in Portsmouth with the Rendezvous still presenting mostly familiar acts on Saturday nights, including the Graham Bond Organisation, the T-Bones, Downliners Sect and Jimmy Powell & the Five Dimensions, while Kimbells' Sunday nights generally continued with its R&B policy. Those Sunday nights gradually relied more frequently on local groups but occasionally there were bigger acts, not least on Sunday 21 February 1965 when the Yardbirds appeared on one of Eric Clapton's last gigs with the band. Just four days later at the same venue, a new club that would have a huge impact on the Portsmouth scene opened its doors. The Birdcage Club opened at first in Kimbells, Osborne Road initially every Thursday, and as it expanded over the summer became an increasing threat to the Rendezvous Club. The first act to appear there was Gary Farr & the T-Bones; Farr's brother Rikki came from Brighton and was one of the key figures in the early days of the Birdcage along with Robin Beste and local DJ Pete 'Brady' Boardman. While the Kimbells R&B Club with links to Southampton's Concorde Club and the Rendezvous Club dating back to 1960 both had roots in the older jazz scene, the ethos of the Birdcage was new, up-to-date and mod, a once exclusive, London phenomenon that was now a far more visible subculture, partly as a consequence of Bank Holiday misdemeanours reported as 'moral panics' in the mass media, but also because through its look and sounds, it became the first significant youth fashion movement of the 1960s.

In the first few months what distinguished the Birdcage from the other local R&B clubs was perhaps rather more 'Brady's' records than the visiting acts, however accomplished, since Chris Farlowe & the Thunderbirds, Ronnie Jones & the Nightimers, the T-Bones, the Sheffields, Zoot Money & the Big Roll Band and the Paramounts were popular, but familiar to local audiences. There were two visiting acts from the USA, New Orleans blues pianist Champion Jack Dupree, the only concession to the older blues styles to appear at the Birdcage, and the briefly 'cool' 'all-girl' band Goldie & the Gingerbreads. In late July however, following a lively appearance on the first Saturday Birdcage night by recent chart-toppers the Moody Blues came a series of events which distinguished the Birdcage and the local mod scene from what had gone before. First came a four-night Birdcage Festival 'Week' with the Shevells on Thursday, Ronnie Jones & his new band the Blue Jays on

Friday, Saturday night with Jimmy James & the Vagabonds, and then on Sunday a one-off relocation for the club to the Savoy Ballroom starring the latest mod's favourites The Who – a legendary night for those involved in the emerging local scene.

The Who already had a certain cult status on London's mod scene, just a month after the release of their second single "Anyway, Anyhow, Anywhere" with the 'B' side a cover of Derek Martin's R&B hit "Daddy Rolling Stone". It would be a further five months before their first album which included covers of two tracks from the influential James Brown album *Live at the Apollo* "I Don't Mind" and "Please, Please, Please", plus Bo Diddley's "I'm a Man" and their third single, "My Generation". Their set list in those days included Howlin' Wolf's "Smokestack Lightnin'", another James Brown song "Shout & Shimmy"; "Heatwave by Martha & the Vandellas and Garnett Mimms' "Tell Me Baby". They would soon become one of the major international rock acts but in the summer of 1965 they were another London-based R&B band, edging towards a fondness for soul and Motown over the older blues. Of their night at the Savoy with 1,000 fans, 'Spinner' in the *Evening News* noted the "sheer noise and visual entertainment' although added, "from the musical point of view it was not of a very high standard".

From 1965 onwards, black artists and music of black origin were to be found in Portsmouth mostly in Guildhall concerts or at The Birdcage, and its successor (from Christmas 1967) the Brave New World. In April 1965, the Guildhall presented the Motown show with the Supremes, Martha & Vandellas, Stevie Wonder, the Miracles, backed by the Earl Van Dyke Six, with British guests Georgie Fame & the Blue Flames, although Portsmouth was not alone in reporting disappointing attendances at a time when Motown and soul was just beginning to rise in popularity. The tour opened at the Finsbury Park Astoria and visited 20 cities but with half empty venues on many nights it became known as the 'Ghost Tour', although it probably paid dividends in the longer term not least because it launched the Tamla Motown label in Britain and all the acts – plus the Temptations – recorded a one hour *Ready Steady Go!* Motown special for ITV. In *the Evening News*, 'Spinner' praised the "superb" show in Portsmouth which he thought "had everything; professionalism … (and) first-class presentation, building to an intense climax", although he added "it would have been even better if people downstairs could have danced".

He suggested further that poor attendances were affecting many of these package tours, citing disappointing crowds recently nationwide for Chuck Berry and PJ Proby and felt that only the Beatles and Rolling Stones were certain to draw full houses. It is worth adding that the Portsmouth show was on a Monday evening, while on the previous Thursday the recently opened Birdcage Club had a large attendance for a double bill of Chris Farlowe & the Thunderbirds and the Brian Auger Trinity, on Friday night the Hollies were at the Savoy, and on Saturday recent chart-toppers the Moody Blues were at the Rendezvous. Rod Watts, keyboard player then with the Academy and the Soul Society and still gigging, remembered it as "the most memorable concert I went to back in the sixties. It's still hard to imagine we were privileged to see so many great artists on one bill".

We do not have a set list from that Motown tour except that on most nights the acts came back together at the end to perform Smokey Robinson's "Mickey's Monkey" There is however a live album from the Paris gig that came after the British tour finished which is probably close to the Portsmouth show. It lists three tracks by the Supremes, "Stop in the Name of Love", "Baby Love", and "Somewhere" from *West Side Story,* plus "Ooo Baby,

Baby" and "Mickey's Monkey" by the Miracles, and "Dancing in the Street", "Nowhere to Run" and Pete Seeger's "If I Had a Hammer" by Martha & the Vandellas. Stevie Wonder added Tommy Tucker's "Hi Heel Sneakers" and Willie Nelson's "Funny How Time Slips Away" to his own "Fingertips, while the Earl Van Dyke Six played their version of the Marvelettes' "Too Many Fish in the Sea".

In the summer of 1965 the Savoy tried briefly to attract the Birdcage and Rendezvous crowd on Monday nights, opening with Georgie Fame & the Blue Flames followed by Them, Goldie & the Gingerbreads, the Yardbirds, the Moody Blues, and Steam Packet. It was not a success and ceased around the same time in August 1965 that the Rendezvous, just after its fifth birthday party starring Manfred Mann, opened for the last time with the newly-formed, jazz-influenced Alan Price Set. The Rendezvous had tried to compete with the Birdcage, sometimes by chang-ing its day of the week and reducing prices to 3/- on occasions but it did not succeed. There were no rockers in evidence, but in the battle *for* the mods, the Birdcage had won and for the next two years it would dominate the live club scene in the city, including visits from a number of black American artists. The announcement that the Rendezvous was closing just months after Graham Bond's record attendance listed some recent attendance figures, with 376 for Manfred Mann, 221 for the return of Graham Bond but down to 80 for Alan Price. At around the same time, shortly after the Birdcage moved to the former Court Ballroom in Eastney, Kimbells closed temporarily for rebuilding.

Six weeks after the Motown show, the black British singer Shirley Bassey returned for her fifth Guildhall concert in five years, appearing with Cyril Stapleton's Orchestra but over the next couple of years, while the clubs shifted towards the sound of sixties soul and Motown, the Guildhall passed on it. There would be folk (Julie Felix, Gordon Lightfoot, the Spinners, Ramblin' Jack Elliott) Pop (Roy Orbison, Lulu, Donovan, Tom Jones, the Troggs, Gene Pitney, the Walker Brothers) jazz and big bands, as well as some British acts that appeared at the clubs such as the Spencer Davis Group, the Small Faces and the Kinks. But the touring American acts either played the smaller Birdcage Club or they went elsewhere – in the 1960s for example, Chuck Berry played in Southampton and Bournemouth but not Portsmouth.

In the mid-1960s, British television, expanding with BBC2 and the ITV regional franchises reflected the growing popularity of sixties soul – not least through the live (as opposed to video) appearances on BBC1's popular show *Top of the Pops* which launched in January 1964 with the Beatles' "I Want to Hold Your Hand" at number one. The majority of artists were always white and disproportionately British, presumably because they were more available to appear, but in April, Millie ("My Boy Lollipop") was the first black artist to appear live, to be followed at intervals that year by older acts Chuck Berry, Louis Armstrong and John Lee Hooker before the Supremes' first appearance in September 1964. Chubby Checker was on the screen in April 1965, then towards the end of the year Wilson Pickett (November) Fontella Bass (December) and Stevie Wonder (January 1966). This (online) list records only *first* appearances so there was another long break before a flurry with Robert Parker ("Barefootin'") and Lee Dorsey in October 1966, Little Richard in November and the initial surprise of the Jimi Hendrix Experience at the end of the year. 1967 brought Otis Redding in March, and PP Arnold in April by which time the contemporary scene in Portsmouth was changing again with the early days of the 'Summer of Love' and the end of the Birdcage.

Prior to that, the weekly *Record Mirror* had listed the British soul/R&B Top Ten which in 1966 opened with "Rescue Me", Don Covay's "See Saw" and Marvin Gaye's "Ain't that Peculiar. A couple of weeks later Joe Tex was at the top with "A Sweet Woman Like You", displaced the following week by Otis Redding's "My Girl". In mid-February Stevie Wonder's "Uptight' was at the top followed by Lee Dorsey ("Get Out of My Life Woman") and "Uptight" was still there in mid-March challenged by Wilson Pickett's "6345789" and James Brown's "I Got You (I Feel Good)". By April 1966, Motown featured strongly with the Four Tops, Marvin Gaye, the Isley Brothers and Stevie Wonder all in the top ten and dancers will have enjoyed the instrumental "You Can't Sit Down" by the Phil Upchurch Combo, denied the number one spot only by Roy C's "Shotgun Wedding". By August's height of the Summer of Love, *Sgt. Pepper* and Scott McKenzie's "San Francisco (Be Sure to Wear Some Flowers in Your Hair)", it was Edwin Starr with "Headline News" who topped the soul charts, followed by the Four Tops' "Loving You is Sweeter than Ever" and Robert Parker's "Barefootin'". The following week, Portsmouth's Birdcage Club closed for final time.

E I G H T

In the Midnight Hour

Wilson Pickett, Ike & Tina Turner, Jimmy James & Vagabonds

B y the second half of the 1960s the biggest audience for black American music in Portsmouth was for what was called 'soul' music. although like jazz and blues the label covered a range of different styles and approaches – and came from a number of different centres. Detroit's Tamla Motown for example aimed at a crossover market and was commercially very successful, while Chicago's Chess Records moved away from what Muddy Waters called the 'Deep Blues' towards its own soul sound; it was less successful on the British pop charts than Motown, although their biggest hit "Rescue Me" by Fontella Bass reached number 11 around Christmas 1965 and was a club favourite among mod dancers. Other Chess acts loved in the clubs included Bobby Womack's Valentinos, who had released the original of "It's All Over Now", Etta James, Tony Clarke, Billy Stewart, and jazz pianist Ramsey Lewis with two memorable instrumentals, "Wade in the Water" and "The In-Crowd". Unlike many of the earlier post-war blues acts, many of their sixties soul singers were women including Chess label's Sugar Pie DeSanto ("Soulful Dress") who appeared at the Birdcage Club in its first Kimbells incarnation. Another black woman singer who appeared at the (Eastney) Birdcage in May 1966 was Dee Dee Warwick, Dionne's sister, who recorded on various labels including Red Bird based in New York, and set up by the (white) songwriters Jerry Leiber & Mike Stoller who wrote for the Coasters, Elvis, the Drifters and many others. Their mid-1960s label had hits with the Shangri-Las, the Dixie Cups, the Ad Libs, and others, including Bessie Banks' original version of the Moody Blues hit "Go Now" and Alvin Robinson's "Something You Got" and "Down Home Girl – the latter covered by the Rolling Stones on their second album.

There is a detailed story to be told elsewhere about a century of black American record releases and the companies that put them out there, not least the role of the major mostly white-owned and run labels, the plethora of smaller independent labels – and the work of white British researchers and fans who through purchases and publications brought them to public attention, whether through the many publications of British academic Paul Oliver, 1960s D-I-Y magazines like *R&B Monthly* and *Soul* or in the 1970s, through the impact of Northern Soul and a few years later the post-*Quadrophenia* Mod revival.

To a large extent 45rpm singles – often imports – were the staple of the new DJs on the 1960s mod club scene but there were notable albums, although some, like James Brown's *Live at the Apollo*, the Impressions' *Big Sixteen* and most of the major Tamla Motown acts were based around previously released singles. The Impressions' album brought together the remarkable work of Curtis Mayfield, after he had replaced Jerry Butler in the vocal trio, with songs like "People Get Ready", "Amen", "We're a Winner", "Meeting Over Yonder" and "Keep on Pushing"; overall, a Chicago-based fusion of gospel, and doo-wop, into soul. A number of Mayfield's songs had a political dimension, which followed Sam Cooke's masterpiece "A Change is Gonna Come", anticipated tracks like James Brown's "Say It Loud – I'm Black and I'm Proud", Aretha Franklin's

"Respect" or a deliberate 'reading' of a song like Ben E King's "Stand by Me" which he sang at the Birdcage in October 1965.

Eventually the southern soul recordings of Stax Records were licensed to Atlantic Records in New York and in Britain it meant that Stax artists like Otis Redding, Arthur Conley ("Sweet Soul Music", Eddie Floyd ("Knock on Wood"), the Bar-Kays ("Soul Finger") and Sam & Dave ("You don't know like I know" & "Hold on I'm Coming") appeared on the same label as Atlantic stars such as Ray Charles, the Coasters, the Drifters and from 1966, Aretha Franklin. None of those Stax artists came to Portsmouth although we were able to enjoy Otis Redding's *Ready Steady Go!* television special featuring Otis Redding with guest spots from Britain's Eric Burdon and Chris Farlowe – the latter a regular Birdcage Club visitor with his band the Thunderbirds.

But Portsmouth did enjoy one of the leading Stax/Atlantic stars of the mid-1960s when Wilson Pickett appeared at the Birdcage in November 1965 on the back of his first British hit "In the Midnight Hour". Over the next three years he would enjoy other top thirty hits, including "Mustang Sally", sung by Pickett in the 1991 movie *The Commitments,* and thereafter an almost obligatory inclusion in the live set of any British R&B band. In addition to Wilson Pickett, Sugar Pie DeSanto, Little Richard and Dee Dee Warwick, other black American acts to appear at the Birdcage included singers who made the original versions of songs that became hits for British acts such as Major Lance ("Um Um Um Um Um"), Lou Johnson ("Always Something there to Remind Me") and Arthur Alexander whose "Anna" was on the first Beatles album and "You Better Move On" was released by the Rolling Stones on their first EP along with tracks by Barrett Strong, Chuck Berry and the Coasters. The Drifters and their former singer Ben E King both played at the Birdcage

– the latter watched by Pete Townshend who said he was "superb" – and also there were three notable black American duos: The Soul Sisters, Charlie & Inezz Foxx ("Mockingbird") and improbably on a Sunday Afternoon in October 1966, the Ike & Tina Turner Revue with the Ikettes. That summer they had enjoyed their top three Phil Spector-produced hit single "River Deep, Mountain High", they had just finished a British tour as the chosen support act to the Rolling Stones, and later that evening played at Hounslow's Ricky Tick Club. One man who played London *instead of* the Birdcage was Bo Diddley; apparently booked for October 1965, with posters all over the city, he stayed in London and appeared at the Flamingo.

When the Birdcage opened in Kimbells, Southsea in February 1965 it relied mostly on British R&B acts like the T-Bones, Chris Farlowe, the Paramounts and Zoot Money's Big Roll Band who reflected a gradual shift from guitar-based R&B to bands with a stronger leaning towards soul and jazz. This had been anticipated pre-Birdcage early in 1964 when Georgie Fame & the Blue Flames were regular visitors to Kimbells R&B nights, while Manfred Mann with strong modern jazz roots were almost a home-grown band, and jazz oriented-bands like Long John Baldry & the Hoochie Coochie Men and the Graham Bond Organisation were very popular at the Rendezvous Club. But following the premature death of Cyril Davies in 1964, the guitar/harmonica bands like the Rolling Stones, Yardbirds, Pretty Things and Kinks either travelled in a 'pop', rock or perhaps psychedelic direction, while others like the once popular Downliners Sect are remembered fondly, but faded away. That left John Mayall's Bluesbreakers, with first Eric Clapton, then Peter Green to fly the flag for the older guitar-based urban blues style but to a fairly large extent dancing drove the musical fashions in the clubs led by the best informed DJs.

There were two somewhat contrasting bands in particular that epitomised that shift at the Birdcage. In mid-July 1965 the club presented for the first time the five-piece guitar-based Action, perhaps *the* cult British mod band who featured accomplished harmonies behind lead singer Reg King and covered soul and Motown tracks, often by the 'girl groups' such as the Marvelettes ("I'll Keep Holding On"), or Martha & the Vandellas ("In My Lonely Room" & "Heatwave") plus "Baby You Got It" (the Radiants), "Since I Lost My Baby" (the Temptations), "Ooh Baby Baby" (the Miracles), "Monkey Time" (Major Lance) "Land of a Thousand Dances" (Chris Kenner) and "Harlem Shuffle" (Bob & Earl). Only one band appeared at the Birdcage Club more often than the Action and that was Jimmy James & the Vagabonds who came first in mid-June 1965 and over the next two years did almost 30 gigs at the club. But while the Action were a white British group signed like the Beatles with George Martin and the Parlophone label, Jimmy James & the Vagabonds had arrived from Jamaica to base themselves in Britain where they played original songs plus covers of the big soul hits of the day.

For Portsmouth, Jimmy James & the Vagabonds went further. Their first album *New Religion* had two sides: 'Mood Red' for dancing and 'Mood Blue' "more serious and a lot more sensitive" including covers of soul favourites like "It's Growing" (Temptations), "Amen" and "People Get Ready" (the Impressions) plus Jimmy's own beautiful "Come to Me Softly". The LP cover showed the band in a Soho street but above it was a photo of them on stage at the Birdcage with local mod Cilla Gilmore and others dancing, while the sleeve notes for this "study in progressive pop" described the impact the band made when it first came to the Birdcage, which left them "nourished" and prompted the album's title *The New Religion*. Subsequently their label Pye, recorded a live album, shared with another favourite Birdcage soul band The Alan Bown Set for which a coach-load of Portsmouth mods travelled to be in the audience – the neon Birdcage sign was in the front cover montage. Decades later Jimmy James was inducted as one of the few 'outsiders' on the Guildhall's 'Wall of Fame'.

When the band first arrived in London they had what would later be known as a ska 'feel' a style which in those early days in Britain was often called Blue Beat after the label on which many of those Jamaican pre-reggae tracks were issued. The label grew from Melodisc which in Britain through the 1950s issued calypso and jazz with a growing client-base of those who had arrived on the Empire Windrush and subsequently. During its two years at the Birdcage the sound of Jimmy James & the Vagabonds was much more in the contemporary American soul field but gradually the club came to acknowledge a growing interest in ska and in its final year, 1967, there were midweek soul and ska record nights at the club plus a live appearance by the mods' favourite Prince Buster. Then in its last month and on its final night Joyce Bond brought her 'Lovers' Rock' sound to the club.

By that time the club had also been presenting acts that would contribute to the British psychedelic sounds – Cream, Pink Floyd (twice), Tomorrow and others – and the Birdcage audience began to split. Some of the mods and other regulars remained committed to black American and Jamaican sounds and also to the post-mod fashions which became more severe, moving towards the skinhead look. Those people mostly moved to the old Ricky's Club, now the Marina, in Goldsmith Avenue where through the 1970s they could dance to a range of sounds including ska and old Birdcage soul favourites. The others – and the choice of drugs was not incidental in the spilt – pursued this new predominantly white experimental and largely self-penned rock and initially called themselves 'Heads' although they tend now to be remembered from the late 1960s and early 1970s as 'Hippies'.

By the late-1960s, local groups, in some cases with the same musicians, had moved from rock & roll and British beat, through blues and rhythm & blues towards the soul sounds of Tamla Motown, Atlantic, Stax, Chess and the British reissues on Guy Stevens' Sue Label. The earliest of these groups locally included the Rampant, the Soul Society and the St Louis Checks – the latter reached the Final of a *Melody Maker* competition in 1966 – but the biggest impact came from the one nationally successful Portsmouth group of the 1960s, Simon Dupree & the Big Sound.

In the earlier R&B days, they had some success locally as the Roadrunners, with regular support gigs at the Rendezvous, before they reformed with the third Shulman brother Phil who brought brass and reeds to the sound, while they introduced the bass player and drummer from the Classics alongside Eric Hine (organ), Derek Shulman (vocals) and Ray Shulman (guitar). Before signing a recording contract and touring nationally they attracted large local crowds to venues like the Indigo Vat in Hampshire Terrace and Thorngate Hall in Gosport, and by 1966 they were touring nationally supporting the Walker Brothers with a set including Don Covay's "Sookie Sookie"; "I'll Put a Spell on You" (Screamin' Jay Hawkins/Nina Simone), "I Don't Mind" (James Brown), "Amen" (the Impressions) and Sam & Dave's "Hold I'm Coming" & "You Don't Know Like I Know". At Christmas 1966, as they moved from local to national professional status, Portsmouth's *Evening News* ran its first of what would become an annual pop poll, where the presence of the Soul Society (8th), and St Louis Checks (9th) indicated a growing fondness for soul bands; they were joined in the following year by the first incarnation of the Inspiration. The Soul Society meanwhile began regular gigs at North End's Oasis Club, renamed on these nights the Soul Parlour, and run by their manager (and local DJ) Lyn Ashton and there were more 'record' nights for dancers replacing live gigs in venues like the original Pomme D'Or, Monday nights at the Mecca, midweek at the Birdcage and elsewhere.

Despite the psychedelic 'Summer of Love', there was another local soul band starting out as 1967 moved towards its final months, Harlem Speakeasy, who by the start of 1968 expanded to add tenor and baritone saxophones, and trumpet to their organ and guitars. At a Guildhall charity gig in late winter 1968, their set, indicative of the kinds of numbers covered by local soul bands at that time, including songs by the Impressions, Junior Walker, the Temptations, Otis Redding, and Edwin Starr. Their performances usually ended with popular soul crowd pleasers like "Amen", "Sock it to 'em JB" and "Land of 1000 Dances", and in the spring they auditioned successfully in London and signed with Polydor Records and the Chrysalis Agency. They released one single, a cover of the Drifters' 'B' side "Aretha", and toured the country's clubs and ballrooms but made little impact, and split in December 1968. One of the relatively few local bands to stay faithful to the soul sound were Image, fronted by singer Phil Freeman, previously with the Soul Society. With local DJ Pete Cross – a veteran of the Birdcage – they offered regular soul gigs at the newly opened Tricorn Centre's club into the 1970s.

On the live club scene the former Birdcage became the Brave New World around Christmas 1967 and, with a licensed bar, unlike the Birdcage, opened with gigs by old favourites Ronnie Jones & the Blue Jays, Jimmy James & the Vagabonds, the Who and a short residency by Harlem Speakeasy. Among a variety of different pop, soul, blues, jazz and cabaret acts through 1968, the club presented American soul acts James & Bobby Purify, PP Arnold, Root 'n' Jenny Jackson and Patti LaBelle & her Blue Bells. The club also booked the Fantastics a soul vocal group from the United States who were based in Britain and caused 'complications' initially by being billed sometimes as the 'Fabulous Temptations' which led to music 'papers publishing a denial from Tamla Motown. They were nonetheless were well-liked at their Portsmouth gigs while the same was apparently not true when a group called 'the Ronettes' appeared at the Locarno and 'Spinner' noted there was "some controversy" as to their "originality". Fortunately when Lee Dorsey appeared there in September 1968 he was the 'real thing'.

The Brave New World took an increasing eclectic approach. The club featured the Amboy Dukes, the Herd and future Woodstock stars Ten Years After; invited Jon Isherwood to run Sunday folk nights with British acts the Singing Postman, Malcolm Price and acoustic blues singers Jo Ann Kelly and Cliff Aungier. There were briefly jazz acts on Monday evenings such as black American singer Dakota Staton, and leading British modernists Stan Tracey and Tubby Hayes, plus Humphrey Lyttleton with singer Elkie Brooks. On the new rock and progressive side, John Peel compered Blossom Toes and Gary Farr, and other 'album' acts included Family, Spooky Tooth, Julie Driscoll and Brian Auger. By the time the Brave New World closed in late September 1968, it was often advertising nothing more than record nights with free entrance and it became a mainstream nightclub, renamed the Pack, by which time fewer British soul acts appeared in Portsmouth.

NINE

Islands in the Sun

Calypso, Millie, Georgie Fame, Prince Buster, Ska

W hen the SS Empire Windrush arrived in Britain in June 1948 it brought a number of musicians from the Caribbean, including from Trinidad the singer known as 'Lord Kitchener' who celebrated his arrival by performing his calypso "London is the Place for Me" *a capella* on the dockside for the Pathé newsreel cameras. Three years later he recorded a version in London with Freddy Grant's Caribbean Rhythm, a session when he also recorded "Kitch's Bebop Calypso" released on Melodisc. Lord Kitchener had arrived along with another Calypso performer, Lord Beginner and they soon found a role entertaining British audiences, including the new arrivals from the Caribbean on the radio and through record releases and live performances.

The Melodisc label began in Britain in 1949, releasing various titles including those licensed by Emile Shalit of the USA's Savoy label. In the early 1950s, Shalit moved to London and started the Blue Beat label which in Britain released new Jamaican recordings, leading to early Ska records often being called 'Blue Beat' in this country. Before this, many of the calypso records were topical, including the London 'arrival' song, "The Underground Train", "Birth of Ghana", and Lord Beginner's recordings with the Calypso Rhythm Kings including "Jamaica

Hurricane". In 1953, in anticipation of the great event, Young Tiger (with Cyril Blake's Calypso Serenaders) recorded "I was there at the Coronation", while one of the best-known songs in Britain was Lord Beginner's "Victory Test Match" (August 1950) describing the match between the England and West Indies cricket teams at Lord's that summer, when West Indies won for the first time in this country. The moment of victory brought great celebrations among the recently-arrived West Indies supporters and the Calypso, praising their two main bowlers included a refrain which ran, "With these little pals of mine, Ramadhin and Valentine". A few days later the tourists came to Southampton to play against the Hampshire county side, attracting a huge crowd and when those two men came again on the next West Indies tour in 1957 the song was revived on British radio and television.

There is no evidence of any of these calypso singers performing in Portsmouth – Lord Kitchener lived mostly in Manchester – but we have noted previously that Mervyn Nelson's production "The Jazz Train" played at the King's Theatre for a week in April 1955 and he made a few changes for the European tour from the production that had run previously in New York including, *the Evening News* recounted, the addition of "a West Indian calypso scene" because Nelson "thought it was a good idea to have music from the islands which are part of the British Commonwealth".

Also during the 1950s, the Jamaican jazz trumpeter and bandleader Leslie 'Jiver' Hutchinson and his 'all coloured band' appeared a number of times in the city at the Savoy, Theatre Royal and Embassy Ballroom. 'Jiver' Hutchinson had played in Jamaica in the 1930s before coming to London where he was a member of a number of bands including those of Ken 'Snakehips' Johnson and Geraldo. He was incidentally a different man from Leslie 'Hutch' Hutchinson from Grenada, a huge international star who spent time in Britain between the wars. We have noted already that the Jamaican saxophonist Joe Harriott was a regular visitor to the city through two decades and his fellow Jamaican Harold McNair (saxophone and flute) played initially at Ricky's with the Arthur Ward Quartet in 1962 and returned to the city shortly after, at the Rendezvous.

From the mid-1950s, Caribbean popular music, especially from Jamaica, enjoyed spells of popularity in the British charts beginning with Harry Belafonte, who was born in Harlem, New York of Jamaican parents. His third album *Calypso* released in 1956 was the first million-selling album by a solo artist and included a hit single "Banana Boat Song (Day-O)" which reached number two in 1957, followed a couple of months later by "Island in the Sun" ("All my days I will sing in praise, of your forest, waters, your shining sand"). This was the theme song from a film of the same name, was from his follow-up album *Belafonte Sings of the Caribbean* and went to number three. The *Calypso* album also included the nostalgic "Jamaica Farewell" ("I must declare my heart is there"). Another black 'folk' singer from New York, Josh White wrote an article for Britain's *Melody Maker* in 1960 in which he praised Belafonte, who he said "can sing a nice ballad" and added that on calypso Belafonte "does something that nobody else has done", while also ensuring "the public could understand them".

There was a brief taste for 'exotic' Mediterranean and African songs and tunes in the British pop charts in the late 1950s and early 1960s and there were also two rather odd 'calypso' records by British comedians that appeared in the lower reaches of the British charts, "Gossip Calypso" by Bernard Cribbins in December 1962 and Lance Percival's cover of "Shame and Scandal in the Family" in October 1965. Percival's use of the calypso form first came to public notice on BBC television's satire show *That Was the Week That Was* (TW3: 1962-1963) when Percival would compose songs about current events. Most pertinently perhaps Elias & his Zig Zag Jive Flutes from South Africa reached number two in April 1958 with the original recording of "Tom Hark", a song which would be covered in a ska style a few years later, as Jamaican songs began to have an influence in Britain.

This was a mixed bag of songs and origins but 1964 marked the year when Jamaican music, particularly early ska, began to have an impact that went beyond the British Caribbean communities. The first impact came from the Jamaican singer Millie (Small) with her 1964 hit "My Boy Lollipop" which reached number two and spent four months in the charts. She appeared three times in Portsmouth in that year, once at the Savoy supported by a local mod R&B group Barry & the Zodiacs, once on a package tour with British chart groups the Dave Clark Five and the Applejacks, and later with the Honeycombs, Lulu and Gene Vincent.

During that same year London group the Migil Five who had started as a jazz outfit enjoyed their one big hit, a ska version of "Mockingbird Hill" which reached number 10 – they played at the Savoy ballroom on Tuesday 5 May – but longer term, and beyond a simple matter of chart positions, a bigger contribution came from Georgie Fame & the Blue Flames, one of the leading London club bands who played quite frequently on the Portsmouth R&B club scene from 1964-1966. Fame's six or seven-piece band explored a broad range of mostly American music including soul songs like "Papa's Got a Brand New Bag", "See Saw", "The Monkey Time", and "Sitting in the Park", instrumentals "Green Onions" "Night Train" and "Last Night", songs from Ray Charles like "Get on the Right Track", "Lil' Darlin'"

(Count Basie), "Parchman Farm" and "I Love the Life I Live" by Mose Allison, and rhythm & blues classic "Let the Good Times Roll". In addition, in 1964 a few months before his number one hit record, "Yeh, Yeh", he released an EP, the title of which was indicative of its sound, *Rhythm & Blue Beat*. The Blue Flames were augmented by trumpeter Eddie Thornton and the four tracks were "Humpty Dumpty", "Madness", "Tom Hark Goes Bluebeat" and "One Whole Year Baby". "Humpty Dumpty" was originally a 1961 Blue Beat release by Eric Humpty Dumpty Morris & the Drumbago All Stars, while "Madness" was originally a Trojan release by the first big ska name in Britain, Prince Buster.

Georgie Fame & the Blue Flames were not a blues band in the 'Chicago' style but they became more involved than other white acts with London's Caribbean audiences. They opened the Roaring Twenties Club where Jamaican Count Suckle was the star DJ, playing dance tunes including jazz and Blue Beat and in addition to Soho's Flamingo they might be found at the Scene and Ram Jam Clubs, the latter south of the river in Brixton. Intriguingly as an organist Georgie Fame was also in London's Advision Studios in 1963 backing Prince Buster on the *Soul of Africa* album, which featured Rico Rodriguez on trombone, almost two decades before his time with the Specials. The album included "Madness".

In the same year, 1964, Jimmy James & the Vagabonds from Jamaica arrived in Britain on their first tour, and enjoyed themselves so much that they stayed and became one of the most popular acts playing in Portsmouth and elsewhere through the second half of the decade. Jimmy James had been a solo star in his native Jamaica where he recorded with Coxsone Dodd, a sound system DJ and one of the leading record producers on the island. In the early 1960s he was persuaded to join with the

Vagabonds, already a working band and they came to England where they recorded their first album for Decca and appeared on the BBC television programmes *Tonight* and *Time Out*.

The Vagabonds' album *Ska Time* is an interesting collection of songs presumably reflecting recent times entertaining Jamaican audiences, mixing soul and ska arrangements with familiar standards and popular songs. The album opens with a ska instrumental of Hoagy Carmichael's "Stardust" and there are similar arrangements of the German children's song "The Happy Wanderer", Herbie Hancock's "Watermelon Man", plus a "Calypso Twist" a couple of years after the height of that dance craze, Fats Domino's "Red Sails in the Sunset" and the Jimmy Reed 12-bar blues "Baby What You Want Me to Do". Twelve months later when they arrived in Portsmouth for their first gig, their repertoire was almost entirely soul-based, with some original songs and covers of recordings by Otis Redding, the Impressions, the Miracles, the Temptations, Willie Mitchell, Tony Clarke and Sam & Dave.

By the time Jimmy James & the Vagabonds first played the (Kimbells) Birdcage club, most of the acts appearing there were similarly 'soulful', including other black singers who had settled in Britain, Ronnie Jones, Herbie Goins and Geno Washington. There were also visiting Americans like Charlie & Inez Foxx, Lou Johnson, Sugar Pie DeSanto and later that year Wilson Pickett, Major Lance and Ben E King, while DJ Pete 'Brady' Boardman kept the dancers entertained with the best soul releases. A couple of years later, in the club's last few months 'Brady' had left and the live acts were more varied. There was a one-off gig for the black British soul act Joe E Young & the Toniks – Joe was actually Colin Young from Barbados who later sang lead with the Foundations – while favourites Geno Washington, Herbie Goins, Jimmy James, Chris Farlowe, the

Action and Georgie Fame still appeared, but the American touring acts rarely came now, while more of the new breed of rock and psychedelic bands were appearing including the Who, the Move, Pink Floyd, Tomorrow ("My White Bicycle"), Denny Laine's Electric String Band and John's Children (including Marc Bolan). The other interesting development began simply with record nights featuring nothing but ska and Blue Beat records attracting an audience sporting post-Mod, pre-skinhead fashions and short hairstyles.

The popularity of the ska club nights was translated into a few live gigs before the club closed at the height of the 'Summer of Love' and more broadly ska began appearing in the British charts. At the Birdcage, the live highlight was Prince Buster & the All Stars who appeared in May 1967, two months after his major hit "Al Capone" entered the charts for the first time on its way to number 18. He arrived the week after the first appearance by the Joyce Bond Show and she was back for two of the last three nights in August with her mix of soul and lovers' rock – a variant of ska, as the sounds of Jamaica moved towards the various kinds of reggae (rock steady, dub etc.) which would become so popular in the 1970s, not least on the back of the international successes of Bob Marley & the Wailers, themselves a Blue Beat recording act in the 1960s.

For those for whom the fashion and musical experiments and excesses of the summer of '67 held little interest there were already a number of albums being released in Britain exploring the music of the Caribbean. In one week in mid-August 1967 the Melody Maker reviewed Club Ska '67 Volume 2, noting "a renewed interest in West Indian music in Britain" and identifying the "hypnotic and infectious" track "Last Train to Skaville" by the Ethiopians. On the same page, a separate review of the album "Rock Steady" suggested the sub-genre was "slightly more subtle than its Ska and Blue Beat brothers" with "gentle voices and calypso-type rhythms", while calypso was reviewed with the album "Dr Kitch", the songs of Lord Kitchener, Mighty Sparrow, Lord Creator and others, including the original version of "Shame and Scandal" by the Wailers.

It is possible that the Jimmy Cliff Show appeared in Portsmouth in the late 1960s, although the evidence is not firm. What is certain is that among the other ska and early reggae singles that appeared in the charts in the late 1960s were "Guns of Navarone" by Beat Cruise visitors the Skatalites (number 38 in April 1967), "Liquidator" by Harry J All Stars (number nine) and "Wonderful World, Beautiful People" by Jimmy Cliff (number six) both in October 1969, plus a number of successes by Desmond Dekker: "007" to number 14 in July 1967, "Israelites" to number one in March 1969 and "It Mek" to number seven in June 1969. The music was obviously popular among the Caribbean community in Britain and its appeal was broadening, although the association with skinheads was sometimes a problem as the 1960s drew to a close.

T E N

Purple Haze

Jimi Hendrix, Albert King, Cream, John Mayall

Among the acts that played at the Birdcage in December 1966 were soul/Tamla-style favourites Jimmy James & the Vagabonds, the Action and the Alan Bown Set, but on the first Saturday of the month Cream made their one appearance in Portsmouth (following an earlier one in Gosport) with a live set that was truncated when Ginger Baker was 'indisposed'. The set they played featured a number of blues songs including "Four Until Late" (Robert Johnson); "Rollin' & Tumblin'" (Baby Face Leroy); "Sitting on Top of the World" (Mississippi Sheiks); "Down in the Bottom" (Howlin' Wolf) and "Cat Squirrell" (Dr Ross). Some of these were pre-war blues but played now in the band's powerful rock sound, anchored by a bass player and drummer who were both experienced jazz musicians and had been members of the Graham Bond Organisation; Bond meanwhile was at the Birdcage on New Year's Eve with the soul/Tamla In Crowd, soon to re-orient themselves as the psychedelic Tomorrow, including Steve Howe (Yes) on guitar and Keith West ("Teenage Opera") on vocals.

Cream's performance that night was rooted in black American music – at the time when Eric Clapton was one of the major figures of the British blues scene – but the manner of the band's playing and some of the other songs indicated a different future, including a collaboration on lyrics with contemporary poet Pete Brown. That new approach would manifest the following week in their single release "I Feel Free" and "NSU", two tracks from their first album *Fresh Cream,* which was released the same day and included original songs and some of the blues tracks from their set, plus Willie Dixon's "Spoonful" and "I'm So Glad" by the idiosyncratic Mississippi blues man Skip James. James had recorded that song and a number of others back in 1931, but disenchanted by their lack of success, he withdrew from the music world until he was rediscovered in the 1960s. He then re-recorded for the Vanguard label, played live to American audiences and came to England in 1967, sharing a bill with Son House, Little Walter and others. Cream meanwhile mimed to the new single on BBC's *Top of the Pops* on 29 December. Unusually for a British blues guitarist, Eric Clapton had recently featured on a top ten album in the British charts with the legendary *Blues Breakers* album as a member of John Mayall's quartet.

John Mayall played in Portsmouth just before Cream in mid-November and a week after that he attended a reception at London's 'Bag O'Nails' club for a new 'British' act featuring a black American guitarist and singer, the Jimi Hendrix Experience, who soon after released their first single, "Hey Joe". By the New Year it was in the charts and making its way to number six, to be followed in March 1967 by "Purple Haze" (number three) and two months later "The Wind Cries Mary" which also reached six. In May 1967 Cream released a new single, two original compositions, "Strange Brew" & "Tales of Brave Ulysses' pointing the move from the blues-based material towards rather more of a psychedelic rock style that would be found on their second album *Disraeli Gears.*

Disraeli Gears appeared in the autumn of 1967 as the Jimi Hendrix Experience embarked on one of the more surprising and last of the old package tours which arrived in Portsmouth for two Guildhall shows on 22 November. The crowded bill consisted of Pink Floyd, the Nice, the Move, Amen Corner and Eire Apparent, and with two houses presumably nobody played for more than about 15/20 minutes but local people still remember it with fondness – it came less than six months after Hendrix played his famous set at the Monterey Festival, although not everyone enjoyed that. One of the major (white) rock critics in the United States, Robert Christgau described Hendrix as "terrible" and "a psychedelic Uncle Tom".

The evening at the Guildhall might have followed the old format, but most of those acts pointed to a new world of psychedelic, progressive and eventually heavy rock – a world in which Hendrix was unusual, especially in Britain, as a black performer, although he brought a wealth of experience playing guitar of the American club circuit in bands from backing Little Richard, BB King, Curtis Knight, the Isley Brothers and others. In addition, however 'psychedelic' he might have been, there are a number of recordings showing his roots and mastery of the blues including "Catfish Blues", "Born Under a Bad Sign", "Mannish Boy" and his best-known, "Red House". He did not play the blues *per se* in Portsmouth but we have a set list from the night with a cover of the Troggs' "Wild Thing", his hit singles "Hey Joe", "Purple Haze", and "The Wind Cries Mary", plus album tracks "Stone Free", "Fire" and Foxy Lady".

It was a first and only Portsmouth appearance for Jimi Hendrix, but it was Pink Floyd's third visit to the city, having appeared at the Birdcage in January and April that year, around the time that their first records were beginning to have an impact. There is no doubt that their Birdcage debut complete with light-show was a shock to the mod audience, more familiar with soul acts and dance records, but it signalled a shift in the music played there and elsewhere, as the 'Summer of Love' unfolded across the country. In mid-August 1967, *the Melody Maker* with a front page reporting the end of Britain's Pirate Radio ships London and Caroline, and a new Rolling Stones single "We Love You", reviewed Arthur Conley's album *Sweet Soul* Music, calling it "a typical workmanlike Atlantic soul album", adding "Soul – now there's a dated word!" As things began to change the *Evening News* ran two full-page features in December 1966 about local problems with drugs, titled "Youth in Chains" and "City's Sinister Secret", then in April 1967 they reported the first court case involving LSD after the suspect was found "semiconscious".

The Move were even more familiar to Birdcage regulars than Pink Floyd, having had a residency in 1966, when they had included soul and Motown covers in their sets, although the publicity urged regulars "Don't miss these hip-happy, swerving, swirling masters of sensationalism". Clearly a quest for authenticity it was not, and sadly by the time they and Pink Floyd returned to Portsmouth with Jimi Hendrix, the Birdcage, having struggled with dwindling audiences had closed for good, although it would re-open for a short while as the Brave New World with a mix of acts and styles – adventurous in some respects but confusing in others. Eventually the central figure in those clubs, Rikki Farr, moved back to Kimbells where, in the late 1960s, he had another spell promoting acts from the new British 'blues' boom such as Led Zeppelin, Ten Years After, Taste, Chicken Shack and Savoy Brown. Unlike the earlier R&B years there were few blues bands in Portsmouth in this period – the most notable was perhaps Blues Convention fronted by Bob Pearce from Southampton. He would become a leading figure on the British blues scene in years to come and this band included drummer Bernie Fox who later recorded with Eric Bibb, and Sherman Robertson, and guitarist Denny Barnes who would join blues band Sam Apple Pie. The *Evening News* also mentioned Riverside and Chicago's Insolence but many of the better-known local bands, Coconut Mushroom, Heaven, Rosemary, Aubrey Small were pursuing psychedelic and progressive styles and increasingly writing their own material, which by the late-1960s was almost obligatory for bands pursuing a professional recording career.

Across the jazz spectrum, Maynard Ferguson's Big Band, singer Jon Hendricks and British 'Trad' star Kenny Ball came to the Guildhall in 1969, while alongside the return of Cliff Richard & the Shadows there were two strong trends; firstly a variety of blues acts including BB King, the older blues styles of John Lee Hooker (twice), Champion Jack Dupree, Sonny Terry & Brownie McGhee, and leading British acts Peter Green's Fleetwood Mac, and John Mayall's Bluesbreakers. There was also an appearance by Albert King in his 40s by then, having once played drums for Jimmy Reed but now a fine electric blues guitarist who recorded for Stax, with the relatively modern sound of Booker T & the MGs backing him. Two years earlier his album of singles contained familiar songs like "Crosscut Saw", "Oh Pretty Woman", "Born Under a Bad Sign" and "The Hunter".

The second trend that grew through 1969 would become the dominant tendency of the next decade in venues like the Guildhall, and South Parade Pier; a clear preference for white acts, many playing increasingly heavy rock or what became known as 'prog', plus a growing number of gentler singer-songwriters. In Portsmouth through 1969 this shift was reflected in visiting white acts like Led Zeppelin, Frank Zappa & the Mothers of Invention, Ralph McTell, Country Joe & the Fish, the Strawbs, Jethro Tull, Fairport Convention, Al Stewart, Family, Pentangle, Ten Years After and Pink Floyd (again).

There were fewer notable jazz gigs around the city and although a growing number of clubs often played black American dance records, fewer soul stars were touring the smaller venues – to some extent Portsmouth fans of jazz, blues and soul had to travel, particularly to London, to see the bigger names. There were however a growing number of festivals to attend, notably for Portsmouth people, three consecutive events on the Isle of Wight, just five miles across the Solent and with a Portsmouth link through the involvement of the most prominent local promoter of those years, Rikki Farr. The 1968 festival lasted just one day/night and featured San Francisco's psychedelic Jefferson Airplane, the Crazy World of Arthur Brown, the Pretty Things, Fairport Convention and a number of other new (white) rock acts – plus two rather contrasting Radio One DJs, Jimmy Saville and John Peel.

The following year's festival featured Bob Dylan & the Band, plus a selection of mainly white British acts such as the Who, Pentangle, Moody Blues, Joe Cocker, Family, Free and the Action, now transformed into the more 'progressive' Mighty Baby. Indo-Jazz Fusions represented the experimental jazz world of Joe Harriott and the brief fashion for Indian sitars and tablas, and there were a number of acoustic or folk acts including Julie Felix, Tom Paxton, Gary Farr plus the only black American on the bill, Richie Havens. 1970 was the enormous event which brought a more varied bill, including at various times Miles Davis the Voices of East Harlem, Sly & the Family Stone; Richie Havens (again) and Jimi Hendrix in one of his last live appearances.

1969's Isle of Wight Festival came just a couple of weeks after what is now the most famous of the large outdoor gatherings of those days – the Woodstock Festival. Richie Havens was the only performer who played there as well as the Isle of Wight, and he was also one of a small number of 'non-white' performers at Woodstock, alongside Sly & the Family Stone, Santana, Ravi Shankar and Hendrix. The music seemed to separating into more clearly defined 'camps' with following 'tribes' of fans. One consequence locally was that Portsmouth would never again see the variety and quality of black musicians such as those who had graced its stages through the 1960s.

At Last

My story ends around 1970, with Jimi Hendrix and Miles Davis across the water on the Isle of Wight. The 1960s were remarkable and I hope lend themselves to this historical account although the acts who appeared were representative rather than comprehensive. We saw and heard Ella Fitzgerald but not Billie Holiday, Muddy Waters but not Sonny Boy Williamson, Miles Davis but not John Coltrane, Wilson Pickett but not Otis Redding, Tina Turner but not Aretha Franklin, the Miracles but not the Impressions. That list might go on but the point has not been to claim Portsmouth saw *everyone,* rather that the range and quality of acts, including some very fine British performers, enabled us to understand the richness of black American and Caribbean music to a depth and complexity never before possible.

By the 1970s Portsmouth had no Birdcage, or Rendezvous, the Savoy had become Nero's night club, South Parade Pier's beautiful ballroom burnt down in 1974 and through that decade and beyond, the Guildhall favoured white acts – rock, pop and singer-songwriter. Very few black artists visited Portsmouth in the 1970s, John Lee Hooker came to the Pier and also supported Mungo Jerry at the Guildhall, a couple of 'Blues Legends' tours came to the Centre Hotel and Students Union, Johnny Mathis and Boney M were at the Guildhall in the late 1970s and as that decade drew to a close there were two very fine nights; Jamaican reggae vocal group Culture, plus Sly and Robbie at the Locarno, and then that first famous Two-Tone tour with the Specials, Madness and Selecter at the Guildhall.

The Specials and Selecter were ska-influenced bands from Coventry as were UB40 and the Beat from Birmingham and they comprised young black and white British-born musicians. Similarly and a little later, Bristol's Massive Attack was a wonderfully creative enterprise by black and white musicians and while Madness were a white London band they were influenced by the music of their fellow black Londoners. Also in the 1970s &1980s came lovers rock, Brit funk (Light of the World, Hi Tension etc.), Jazzy B and Soul II Soul plus younger black British jazz musicians like Courtney Pine and Steve Williamson. There is today a new generation of creative British jazz musicians such as the remarkable Sons of Kemet led by Shabaka Hutchings or the many musicians who have graduated through the 'Tomorrow's Warriors' programme in London..

In the years since 1970 perhaps the most interesting Portsmouth musician in the context of this publication was also the most successful, Joe Jackson, whose first hit and first album were released in 1979. His early achievements might be seen more in the context of what is often called 'post punk' or 'new wave' alongside Elvis Costello, Ian Dury and others, but Jackson, a highly accomplished musician, has always pursued jazz influences and links, sometimes in terms of image but also through the music; an obvious example is his self-penned album *Body & Soul* (1984) with its jazz standard title, visual homage to a Blue Note cover and a sound described as a mix of pop, jazz and Latin. A more recent album, *The Duke* features ten Duke Ellington tracks as a tribute to the great composer including "Caravan", "Take the A Train", "Perdido/Satin Doll" and "Mood Indigo". Joe Jackson has a home base in the city and is still an active musician in Britain, Europe and the USA.

Despite Joe Jackson and the occasional event like the big Blues Festival on Southsea Common in 1993, as far as Portsmouth is concerned it seems so much now happened elsewhere. From 1945-1970, visiting black musicians who came here encountered a predominantly white audience; for the most part they were sympathetic and supportive but unlike London, Birmingham, Coventry, Bristol and elsewhere there has never been a large black population in Portsmouth – and in particular very few Afro-Caribbean and Afro-Americans. The 'Windrush' generation did not to any large extent settle here and as many of the big names in black American music died or stopped touring widely, the local music scene, audiences and musicians gravitated to white rock and pop. The one exception has perhaps been in the clubs where there are still DJs who play the best of black dance music, but I am not sure it is mere nostalgia to look back and suggest that in Portsmouth, things ain't (quite) what they used to be.

Appendix

Main Venues & Clubs

BIRDCAGE CLUB	1965-1967, opened in Kimbells, Southsea then moved to Eastney.
BRAVE NEW WORLD	Replaced the Birdcage Club 1968.
CELLAR CLUB	Hampshire Terrace early 1960s traditional jazz, became Indigo Vat
COBDEN ARMS	Arundel Street, (mainly traditional) jazz.
GUILDHALL	Bombed 1941, re-opened 1959, concerts, all genres through 1960s.
KIMBELLS BALLROOM	Osborne Road, Southsea. Sunday R&B 1964, 1965 & 1969.
KING'S THEATRE	Albert Road, jazz, folk concerts and shows
PURE DROP	Middle Street, (mainly traditional) jazz
RAILWAY HOTEL	behind Fratton Station: jazz, folk, R&B, rock & roll.
RENDEZVOUS CLUB	Traditional jazz 1960-1963, Ashburton Rd, SP Pier, Onslow Road
RENDEZVOUS CLUB	R&B 1964-1965, Oddfellows Hall, Kingston Road.
RICKY'S CLUB	Goldsmith Avenue opposite station, jazz, rock & roll, dancing.
SAVOY BALLROOM	Southsea seafront, 1950s dance & jazz bands, 1960s mainly pop.
SOUL PARLOUR	North End junction, mainly soul, then as the Parlour, rock & pop.
SOUTH PARADE PIER	Opposite the Savoy, dance & jazz bands 1950s & early 1960s.
STAR INN	Lake Road, jazz & folk.
SUNSHINE INN	Farlington, (mainly modern) jazz
THEATRE ROYAL	Guildhall Walk, concerts & variety shows.

Diary of Some Major Portsmouth Gigs

1955

April   "The Jazz Train at the King's Theatre (one week)

1956

14 March   Stan Kenton Orchestra from USA in concert at the Savoy Ballroom

10 September   Tony Crombie & his Rockets national debut at the Theatre Royal.

1959

8 June   HM Queen Elizabeth II opens the rebuilt Guildhall

9 June   Chris Barber Jazz Band with Ottilie Patterson at the Guildhall

21 September   The Dave Brubeck Quartet, the Dizzy Gillespie Quintet, Buck Clayton's All-Stars, Jimmy Rushing at the Guildhall

18 October   Kid Ory and his New Orleans Jazz Band at the Guildhall

6 December   The Modern Jazz Quartet plus Ronnie Ross and Joe Harriott at the Guildhall

1960

19 January   The Platters at the Guildhall

28 January   Sarah Vaughan with the Johnny Dankworth Orchestra at the Guildhall

17 March   Ella Fitzgerald, with Jimmy Guiffre at the Guildhall

3 April   Paul Robeson at the Guildhall

24 April   Chris Barber Band with Ottilie Patterson and Sister Rosetta Tharpe at the Guildhall

25 September   Miles Davis Quintet & the Jazz Five at the Guildhall

| 1 December | 'Jazz at the Philharmonic' Dizzy Gillespie, Coleman Hawkins, Benny Carter; Cannonball Adderley Quartet at the Guildhall |

1961

23 March	Ella Fitzgerald and Oscar Peterson Trio at the Guildhall
1 October	Modern Jazz Quartet at the Guildhall
1962	
5 April	Count Basie and Lambert, Hendricks & Ross at the Guildhall
3 May	Louis Armstrong at the Guildhall
10 October	George Shearing, Joe Williams, Junior Mance Trio at the Guildhall
29 November	Dave Brubeck Quartet at the Guildhall
16 December	Chris Barber with Louis Jordan at the Guildhall

1963

14 March	Ella Fitzgerald and Oscar Peterson at the Guildhall
31 March	The Beatles at the Guildhall
24 April	Gerry Mulligan and Bob Brookmeyer at the Guildhall
September	The Rolling Stones at the Savoy Ballroom

1964

January	Kimbells R&B opens with Georgie Fame & Blue Flames residency
3 February	The Tommy Dorsey Orchestra with Frank Sinatra Junior at the Guildhall
8 February	Rendezvous R&B opens at Oddfellows Hall with Jimmy Powell & 5 Dimensions

30 April	American Folk Blues and Gospel Caravan with Muddy Waters, Otis Spann, Cousin Joe Pleasants, Rev. Gary Davis, Sister Rosetta Tharpe, Sonny Terry & Brownie McGhee, at the Guildhall 11 June: John Lee Hooker + Chris Farlowe at Kimbells
21 July	The Ray Charles Orchestra and Raelets at the Guildhall
19 September	Little Walter & John Lee's Groundhogs at the Rendezvous
1 November	Dionne Warwick, the Isley Brothers, with the Searchers at the Guildhall
7 November	Jimmy Reed at Kimbells

1965

21 February	The Yardbirds with Eric Clapton and the J Crow Combo at Kimbells.
15 March	Jesse Fuller, at Clarence Pier
12 April	'Motown' show with Supremes, Martha & Vandellas, Stevie Wonder, the Miracles, Earl Van Dyke Six and guests Georgie Fame & the Blue Flames at the Guildhall
12 June	Rev Gary Davis, Josh White, Buffy Sainte Marie at the Guildhall
1 July	Jimmy James & the Vagabonds first appearance at the Birdcage (first of 29)
17 July	The Rolling Stones, Walker Brothers, and Steam Packet at the Guildhall
28 October	Ben E King at the Birdcage
23 November	Wilson Pickett at the Birdcage

1966

27 January	The Drifters at the BIrdcage
17 April	Arthur Alexander at the Birdcage

18 September	Modern Jazz Quartet at the Guildhall
27 September	Wingy Manone at the Guildhall
11 October	Bud Freeman & Alex Welsh at the Guildhall
16 October	Ike & Tina Turner Revue (afternoon) at the Birdcage
6 November	Ed Hall & Alan Elsdon at the Guildhall
25 November	Little Richard at the Birdcage
3 December	Cream at the Birdcage

1967

5 February	Duke Ellington Orchestra at the Guildhall
10 March	"Jazz from the Swinging Era", Bud Freeman, Earl Hines, Buck Clayton at the Guildhall
14 April	Nina Simone at the Guildhall
13 May	The Joyce Bond Show at the Birdcage
20 May	Prince Buster & the All Stars at the Birdcage
22 November	Jimi Hendrix Experience, the Pink Floyd, the Move at the Guildhall

1968

June	James & Bobby Purify at the Brave New World
August	The Skatalites on the Harbour Beat Cruise
2 October	Oscar Peterson Trio at the Guildhall
November	Sunday Blues Club opens at Kimbells (Led Zeppelin, Taste, Free, Chicken Shack etc.)

1969

12 February	John Lee Hooker, Champion Jack Dupree, Jo-Ann Kelly at the Guildhall
25 April	BB King, Fleetwood Mac, Sonny Terry & Brownie McGhee at the Guildhall
10 November	Albert King and John Lee Hooker at the Guildhall
18 November	John Mayall at the Guildhall

Bibliography

The books, and one or two CDs listed here are mostly those I used in this project. There are many others out there, including biographies of Ray Charles, Nina Simone, plus books about ska to which I didn't have access. While I have indicated their particular relevance to specific chapters, in some cases there will be an overlap to other chapters.

Many of the books mentioned are quite old now, although some (e.g. LeRoi Jones or Paul Oliver might be considered 'Classics'). They are perhaps interesting partly because they emerged around the time that I have been writing about.

Overall the most relevant source was often our local 'paper, the Portsmouth *Evening News* which is available at the main Library. There is also a 'Pompey Pop' Archive available there.

General (Histories of 1950s/1960s)

Andrew Cook, 2013, *1963: That Was the Year that Was*

Simon Hall, 2016, *1956: The World in Revolt*

Peter Hennessy, 2019, *Winds of Change: Britain in the Early Sixties*

David Kynaston, 2013, *Modernity Britain, Opening the Box, 1957-1959*

David Kynaston, 2014, *Modernity Britain, A Shake of the Dice, 1959-1962*

Arthur Marwick, 1998, *The Sixties*

Lynda Nead, 2017, *The Tiger in the Smoke*

Dominic Sandbrook, 2005, *Never had it so Good: 1956-1963, from Suez to the Beatles*

Dominic Sandbrook, 2006, *White Heat: 1964-1970, Britain in the Swinging Sixties*

General (Music)

Theo Cateforis (editor) 2007, *The Rock History Reader* (includes Motown, Pickett, Hendrix, Reggae)

Donald Clarke, 1995, *The Rise & Fall of Popular Music*

Paul du Noyer, 2010, *In the City: A Celebration of London Music*

Mary Ellison, 1989, *Extensions of the Blues*

Ted Gioia, 2011, *The History of Jazz*

LeRoi Jones, 1963, *Blues People*

Allen Lowe, 1997, *American Pop: from Minstrel to Mojo on Record 1893-1956*

Barry McRae, 1987, *The Jazz Handbook*

Paul Oliver, 1997 (2nd ed.) *The Story of the Blues*

Catherine Parsonage, 2005, *The Evolution of Jazz in Britain 1880-1935*

Eileen Southern, 1983 (2nd ed.), *The Music of Black Americans: A History*

Local (Music)

Dave Allen & Mick Cooper, 2011, *Dave & Mick's Pompey Pop Pix*

Dave Allen & Mick Cooper, 2020, *More Pompey Pop Pix*

Dave Allen, 2009, *Here Come the Sixties*

Sharon Lee, John Stedman & Katy Ball, 2003, *'Singing Out: Voices of Portsmouth Rock & Pop Musicians'*

Alan Zeffert, 1988, *Past a Joke: Living, Loving, Laughing, Loafing in Post-War Portsmouth*

1. **Louis Armstrong, 'Kid' Ory, Fats Waller, The British Revival**

    Laurence Bergreen, 1997, *Louis Armstrong: An Extravagant Life*

    Thomas Brothers, 2014, *Louis Armstrong: Master of Modernism*

    Pete Frame, 2007, *Restless Generation: How Rock Music changed the Face of 1950s Britain*

    Walter Hanlon, 2008, *1950s Jazz in London & Paris*

    Jazz in Britain 1919-1950 (4 x CD and Booklet)

    Jim Godbolt, 1984, *A History of Jazz in Britain: 1919-1950*

    George Melly, 1970, *Owning Up*

    Francis Newton, 1960, *The Jazz Scene* (includes 'The British Jazz Fan')

    Mike Pointon & Ray Smith, 2010, *Goin' Home: The Uncompromising Life & Music of Ken Colyer.*

2. **Ellington, Fitzgerald, Basie, The Big Bands**

    Harvey G Cohen, 2010, *Duke Ellington's America*

    Bruce Crowther & Mike Pinfold, 1986, *The Jazz Singers: From Ragtime to New Wave*

    Benny Green, 1989, *Let's Face the Music: The Golden Age of Popular Song*

    Colin King, 2002, *In the Mood: The Kings of the Big Bands*

    Jazz Journal and Jazz & Blues, July 1974, vol. 27, no 7: "Ellingtonian" (tribute issue)

3. **Sister Rosetta Tharpe, Rev. Gary Davis, Josh White, Muddy Waters**

    Bruce Bastin, 1971, *Crying for the Carolines*

Joe Boyd, 2006, *White Bicycles: Making Music in the 1960s.*

Billy Bragg, 2017, *Roots, Radicals & Rockers: How Skiffle Changed the World*

Paul Oliver, 2009, *Barrelhouse Blues: Location Recording & the Early Traditions of the Blues*

Robert Gordon, 2002, *Can't Be satisfied: The Life & Times of Muddy Waters*

Sandra B Tooze, 1997, *Muddy Waters: The Mojo Man*

4. **Louis Jordan, Little Richard, Ray Charles, Nina Simone**
   Nik Cohn, 1969, *Awopbopaloobop Alopbamboom: Pop from the Beginning*

   Peter Guralnick, 1971, *Feel Like Going Home: Portraits in Blues & Rock 'n' Roll*

   Nick Tosches, 1991, *Unsung Heroes of Rock 'n' Roll: The Wild Years Before Elvis*

5. **Miles Davis, Dizzy Gillespie, Sarah Vaughan, Joe Harriott, Roland Kirk**
   Scott DeVaux, 1997, *The Birth of Bebop: A Social and Musical History*

   The Joe Harriott Story (4 x CD and Booklet, Proper Records)

   Duncan Heining, 2012, *Trad Dads, Dirty Boppers & Free Fusioneers*

   Ashley Kahn 2000, *Kind of Blue: The Making of the Miles Davis Masterpiece*

   Eric Nisenson, 2000, *The Making of Kind of Blue: Miles Davis & his Masterpiece*

   Ronnie Scott with Mike Hennessy, 2004 (2nd ed.) *Some of my Best Friends are the Blues*

6. **BB King, John Lee Hooker, Jimmy Reed, Little Walter, British R&B**

    Bob Brunning, 1995 (2nd ed.) *The Blues in Britain; The History 1950s to the Present*

    Leslie Fancourt, 1989, *British Blues on Record 1957-1970: A Selected Discography*

    Christopher Hjort, 2007, *Strange Brew: Eric Clapton & the British Blues Boom 1965-1970*

    Charles Keil, 1966, *Urban Blues*

    Paul Myers, 2007, *It Ain't Easy: Long John Baldry & the Birth of the British Blues*

    Giles Oakley, 1976, *The Devil's Music*

    Mike Rowe, 1973, *Chicago Breakdown*

    Greg Russo, *2011, Mannerisms: The Five Phases of Manfred Mann*

    Harry Shapiro, 1996, *Alexis Korner, the Biography*

7. **The Platters, Drifters, Beatles, Tamla Motown**

    Charlotte Greig, 1989, *Will You Still Love Me Tomorrow*

    David Olusoga, 2016, *Black and British: A Forgotten History*

    Jacqueline Warwick, 2007, *Girl Groups, Girl Culture: Popular Music & Identity in the 1960s*

    Craig Werner, 1998, *A Change is Gonna Come: Music, Race and the Soul of America.*

8. **Wilson Pickett, Ike & Tina Turner, Jimmy James & the Vagabonds**

    Paul Anderson, 2013, *Mods: The New Religion, the Style & Music of 1960s Mods*

Robert Gordon, 2013, *Respect Yourself: Stax Records & the Soul Explosion*

Peter Guralnick, 2002, *Sweet Soul Music.*

9. *Calypso, Millie, Georgie Fame, Prince Buster, Blue Beat & Ska*

Lloyd Bradley 2012 *Bass Culture: When Reggae Was King*

London is the Place for Me: Trinidadian Calypso in London 1950-1956 (CD & booklet on Honest Jons Records)

Uli Twelker, 2014, *Georgie Fame: There's nothing else to do.*

10. *Jimi Hendrix, Albert King, Cream, John Mayall*

Ray Foulk, 2016, *The Last Great Event with Jimi Hendrix & Jim Morrison*

Charles Shaar Murray, 2012, *Crosstown Traffic and Postwar Pop*

Printed by Printforce, United Kingdom